*Lovingly dedicated to
a faithful prayer team:
Charette, Karen, Madalene,
Nancy, Win.*

LIFE MESSAGES OF GREAT CHRISTIANS SERIES
Compiled by Judith Couchman

A Very Present Help
Amy Carmichael

Growing Deeper with God
Oswald Chambers

Loving God with All Your Heart
Andrew Murray

Anywhere He Leads Me
Corrie ten Boom

Dare to Believe
Smith Wigglesworth

Also by Judith Couchman
The Woman Behind the Mirror
Shaping a Woman's Soul
Designing a Woman's Life Bible Study
Designing a Woman's Life
Lord, Please Help Me to Change
Lord, Have You Forgotten Me?
Why Is Her Life Better Than Mine?
If I'm So Good, Why Don't I Act That Way?
Getting a Grip on Guilt

ANYWHERE HE LEADS ME

LIFE MESSAGES OF
GREAT CHRISTIANS

Anywhere He Leads Me

CORRIE TEN BOOM

Compiled by
JUDITH COUCHMAN

SERVANT PUBLICATIONS
ANN ARBOR, MICHIGAN

Vine Books is an imprint of Servant Publications especially designed to serve evangel-ical Christians.

Excerpts from *The Hiding Place* by Corrie ten Boom with John and Elizabeth Sherrill, © 1971, were used by permission of Chosen Books, Inc., Chappaqua, New York. All rights reserved.

Excerpts from *Tramp for the Lord* by Corrie ten Boom © 1974, were used by per-mission of Fleming H. Revell, a division of Baker Book House, Grand Rapids, Michigan. All rights reserved.

Unless otherwise noted, the Scripture verses are taken from the HOLY BIBLE, NEW INTERNATIONAL VERSION. © 1973, 1978, 1984 by International Bible Society. Used by permission of Zondervan Publishing House. All rights reserved. Verses marked NRSV are from the New Revised Standard Version of the Bible, © 1989 by the Division of Christian Education of the National Council of Churches of Christ in the USA. Used by permission. All rights reserved. Verses marked KJV are from the King James Version.

Published by Servant Publications
P.O. Box 8617
Ann Arbor, Michigan 48107

Cover design: Hile Illustration and Design, Ann Arbor, Michigan

00   10 9 8 7 6 5 4 3

Printed in the United States of America
ISBN 1-56955-000-X

LIBRARY OF CONGRESS CATALOGING-IN-PUBLICATION DATA

Ten Boom, Corrie.
Anywhere He leads me / Corrie ten Boom ; compiled by Judith Couchman.
    p.   cm. — (Life messages of great Christians ; 4)
Includes bibliographical references.
ISBN 1-56955-000-X
1. Ten Boom, Corrie—Meditations.   2. Christian biography—Netherlands.
I. Couchman, Judith.   II. Title.   III. Series.
BR1725.T35A3 1997
269'.2'092—dc21
[B]   97-1530
                                                              CIP

Contents

Acknowledgments

MANY THANKS TO Bert Ghezzi, editorial vice president at Servant Publications, for supporting me and the *Life Messages of Great Christians* series. And to Willard Stone at Christian Literature Crusade for researching and granting the rights to Corrie ten Boom's works.

I'm grateful this manuscript passed through the capable hands of Liz Heaney as developmental editor and Traci Mullins as copy editor. Thanks to them for their expertise, encouragement, and friendship. My sister Shirley Honeywell also deserves recognition for her word-processing assistance during a busy deadline season. Thanks, Shirley, for accomplishing what only an older sister would do.

I'm also indebted to my prayer team. Along with my mother Opal Couchman, her friend Mae Lammers, and my sister Shirley, these women prayed for this book: Charette Barta, Win Couchman, Madalene Harris, Karen Hilt, and Nancy Lemons.

Introduction

~

COLOR DRAINED FROM *the man's face. He took a step back from me. "Miss ten Boom! I do hope you're not involved with any of this illegal concealment... It's just not safe! Think of your father!"*

I pulled the coverlet back from the baby's face. The man bent forward, his hand in spite of himself reaching for the tiny fist curled round the blanket. For a moment I saw compassion and fear struggle in his face. Then he straightened. "No. Definitely not. We could lose our lives for that Jewish child!"

Unseen by either of us, Father had appeared in the doorway. "Give the child to me, Corrie," he said.

Father held the baby close, his white beard brushing its cheek, looking into the little face with eyes as blue and innocent as the baby's.... "You say we could lose our lives for this child. I would consider that the greatest honor that could come to my family." [1]

Since childhood Corrie ten Boom walked with Jesus. She credited this relationship to a father who modeled living and dying for their Savior. When the German army began slaughtering Dutch Jews, Papa ten Boom didn't hesitate to harbor fugitives in his modest home, affectionately called the Beje. That decision ignited *The Hiding Place* legacy, a holocaust story of love and forgiveness that for decades has touched millions of people.

Nazi soldiers arrested the compassionate watchmaker and his family, directing them to the dreaded concentration camps. Later when Corrie emerged from imprisonment alive, the faith of her father's family burned within. "We must go everywhere," her

11

sister Betsie had whispered before dying at Ravensbruck. "We must tell people that no pit is so deep that He is not deeper still. They will believe us, because we were here." [2] With her sister's words as inspiration, Corrie decided she could go anywhere with Jesus.

Soon after her release Corrie began "going everywhere." Into her 80s she indefatigably traveled worldwide, telling her story and teaching about God's faithfulness. One of Corrie's primary messages centered on our need to forgive, no matter how horrendous the offense, and she practiced this principle herself.

Eventually Corrie returned to Germany—a difficult step for obvious reasons. At a meeting in a friend's house she noticed a woman who would not look her in the eye. Corrie asked her hostess about the woman and discovered she had worked as a nurse at Ravensbruck. Suddenly Corrie recognized the woman, and was filled with hate. Ten years before, Corrie had escorted Betsie to the camp's hospital barracks. Betsie's feet were paralyzed and Corrie knew her sister was dying. However, the nurse expressed no sympathy and scolded Betsie.

During the meeting Corrie wrestled with her decade-old bitterness and finally asked God for forgiveness. She wanted to fulfill His purposes. The next day, with a supernatural love welling from within, Corrie telephoned the woman and invited her to another session that night.

"What? Do you want *me* to come?" gasped the nurse.

"Yes," replied Corrie. "That is why I called you."

"Then I'll come."

That night during the meeting the nurse looked Corrie directly in the eye and afterward committed her life to Christ.

Corrie faced similar experiences on several occasions and explained the phenomenon: "I, who have kept in my subconscious feelings of hatred, the Lord now uses as a window through which His light can shine into [a] dark heart: His channel for streams of living water." [3]

Aside from embodying God's love and forgiveness, Corrie also talked to audiences about the Bible, prayer, obedience, spiritual victory, service, and the end times. She spoke simply and directly, using personal stories and homespun comparisons to illustrate eternal truths. Some of those stories, excerpted from her lesser-known books, fill this 40-day devotional so that, inspired by Corrie's life and lessons, you can go anywhere He leads you.

—Judith Couchman
April 1996

1. Corrie ten Boom with John and Elizabeth Sherrill, *The Hiding Place* (Old Tappan, NJ: Spire Books, 1971).

2. *The Hiding Place*, 217.

3. Corrie ten Boom, *Not Good If Detached* (Fort Washington, PA: Christian Literature Crusade, 1957), 18. This telling adapted from Judith Couchman, *Designing a Woman's Life* (Sisters, OR: Multnomah Press, 1995), 31-32.

PART ONE

THE WORD AS A GUIDE

There were only two employees in the watch shop in 1898,
the clock man and Father's young apprentice-errand boy.
When Mama had poured their coffee,
Father put on his rimless spectacles and began to read:
"Thy word is a lamp unto my feet,
and a light unto my path....
Thou art my hiding place and my shield:
I hope in thy word...."
What kind of hiding place, I wondered idly
as I watched Father's brown beard rise and fall with the words.
What was there to hide from?

THE HIDING PLACE

CORRIE TEN BOOM'S INSIGHT
When we need its safety, God's Word is a place to hide.
When we desire direction, God's Word is a guide.

THE WORD IS POWERFUL

THOUGHT FOR TODAY

More than we can imagine, God's Word powerfully influences people.

WISDOM FROM SCRIPTURE

Blessed are they whose ways are blameless,
   who walk according to the law of the Lord.
   Blessed are they who keep his statutes
      and seek him with all their heart.
They do nothing wrong; they walk in his ways.
You have laid down precepts that are to be fully obeyed.
Oh, that my ways were steadfast in obeying your decrees!
Then I would not be put to shame
      when I consider all your commands.
I will praise you with an upright heart
      as I learn your righteous laws.
I will obey your decrees; do not utterly forsake me.
How can a young man keep his way pure?
      By living according to your word.
I seek you with all my heart;
      do not let me stray from your commands.
I have hidden your word in my heart
      that I might not sin against you.
For the word of God is living and active. Sharper than any double-edged sword, it penetrates even to dividing soul and spirit, joints and marrow; it judges the thoughts and attitudes of the heart.

—PSALMS 119:1-11; HEBREWS 4:12, NIV

"The Sword of the Spirit which is the Word of God" is far more powerful than our own arguments. We were sitting on the verandah of a university dormitory and a Mrs. Jameson was commenting on the lecture I had given only a few moments before.

"What you just told the students was very interesting, but I do not think you are right. Please do not take it ill of me, but I have had a wider experience than you," she said. "I am a member of an association that has taken me all over the world, and I have talked with outstanding persons in India, Arabia, Japan, and many other countries. I have discussed the road of life through time and eternity with Mohammedans, Brahmins, Shintoists, and many others. There were excellent people among them who came to know God without Jesus Christ. You told the students so positively that we need Him, but that is not true."

"Your argument is not with me, but with the Bible," I said. "It is not I who says so, but the Bible. Jesus said, 'No man cometh unto the Father but by me'" (John 14:6, KJV).

I felt somewhat abashed. A sense of inadequacy often comes over me when I talk with people who are so much better informed than I. At such times this work seems much too difficult for me. Later I talked it over with a friend who said, "You should not try to be anything but an open channel for the Spirit of God. You never can be anything else, even though you may think so at times. Follow the pathway of obedience, and you will be used by God far beyond your own powers."

A reception was being held in Ottawa, Canada, for all who wished to meet H.R.H. Prince Bernhard of the Netherlands. It was a pleasure to see so many Hollanders together. The Prince looked tired, but was cheerful and kind to everyone who addressed him. Photographers surrounded him as they took pictures of him from all sides, in conversation with some important person, or with a sweet country child in his arms.

I met many old acquaintances. And then suddenly I was face to face with Mrs. Jameson.

"I am glad to see you," she said. "You know, I just cannot forget what you said to me when you spoke at our university. Jesus said, 'No man cometh unto the Father but by Me.' I keep thinking about that."

"How wonderful!" I said. "You have listened to the voice of God. Now go on listening and read the Bible. He still has much more to say to you."

The Word of God is living and powerful.

—*Amazing Love*

QUESTIONS TO CONSIDER
1. How have you known God's Word to be living and powerful?
2. How are you allowing God's Word to influence you now?

A PRAYERFUL RESPONSE
Lord, please make Your Word living and powerful in my life. Amen.

THE BIBLE IS FOR YOU

THOUGHT FOR TODAY
We can embrace the Bible's message as our own.

WISDOM FROM SCRIPTURE
If your law had not been my delight,
    I would have perished in my misery.
    I will never forget your precepts,
    for by them you have given me life.
I am yours; save me, for I have sought your precepts.
The wicked lie in wait to destroy me,
    but I consider your decrees.
I have seen a limit to all perfection,
    but your commandment is exceedingly broad.
Oh, how I love your law!
    It is my meditation all day long.
Your commandment makes me wiser than my enemies,
    for it is always with me.
I have more understanding than all my teachers,
    for your decrees are my meditation.
I understand more than the aged,
    for I keep your precepts.
I hold back my feet from every evil way,
    in order to keep your word.
I do not turn away from your ordinances,
    for you have taught me.
How sweet are your words to my taste,
    sweeter than honey to my mouth!
Through your precepts I get understanding;
    therefore I hate every false way.

Your word is a lamp to my feet and a light to my path.
I have sworn an oath and confirmed it,
   to observe your righteous ordinances.

—PSALMS 119:92-106, NRSV

INSIGHTS FROM CORRIE TEN BOOM:

I was again in a German concentration camp for women. In the camp I encountered *Aufseherinnen,* women guards from Ravensbruck, where I had been imprisoned.

I had come here to show these people the way to real freedom. I had come to speak of the love of God that passes all understanding, to tell about Jesus Christ, who came into this world to make people happy under all circumstances.

In one of the factory barracks they were sitting in front of me. Each one had brought a chair from her own dormitory barracks. Their faces were glum, and it seemed as if I were addressing a stone wall.

After having spoken in this camp twice, I consulted the superintendent. "Can you tell me why I get no response at all?"

She laughed and answered, "The women have said to me, 'This Dutch woman speaks in such a simple way. We Germans are more highly cultivated and so much more profound in our theology.' I'm afraid you won't get along too well together. But why don't you try once more? You have permission to speak three times."

When I got home, I went down on my knees. "Lord, won't You please give me a message?" I prayed. "I'm not cultured enough, and not profound enough theologically for these National-socialistic women."

And then came the answer: *Chocolate.* It made no sense to me. Would you call that a message? But suddenly I caught on. I had in my possession a box of chocolates, something not on the market anywhere in Germany, to say nothing of a concentration camp.

The next day I set out for camp full of new courage. There they were, sitting once more in front of me, resistance and distaste on every somber face. But I said, "This is my last visit with you, and so I brought you a little treat—chocolate."

How those faces lit up! What a luxury a piece of chocolate was to those poor prisoners! All at once we were friends. Some of them even asked me to write my name and address in their Bibles.

When I began to speak, I said, "No one has said anything to me about the chocolate. No one asked whether it had been manufactured in Holland or what quantities it contained of cocoa, sugar, milk, or vitamins. You have done exactly what I intended you to do: you have eaten and enjoyed it."

Then I took up my Bible and said, "It is just the same with this Book. If I read about the Bible in a scientific, theological or scholarly way it does not make me happy. But if I read that 'God so loved the world that He gave His only begotten Son, that whosoever believeth in Him should not perish, but have everlasting life' (John 3:16, KJV), then I am really happy."

God's Spirit was working. Barriers fell away and understanding and longing were born in the eyes before me, a hunger to hear more of that love that passes all understanding.

Many months later I was in a large hospital. An emaciated patient seemed to recognize me.

"Don't you remember me?" she asked. "Last year I was a prisoner in Darmstadt," she said. "When you visited the camp, you preached on chocolate. That was the moment of my conversion. Since then I have not read *about* the Bible but *in* it. Now I have to die, but I am not afraid. I have read in His Book that in my Father's house are many mansions. And this I know: Jesus is preparing one also for me."

—*Amazing Love*

QUESTIONS TO CONSIDER
1. Do you just know about the Bible, or do you live it? Why?
2. In what ways can you apply the Bible's principles to your life today?

A PRAYERFUL RESPONSE:
Lord, thank You that the Bible was written for me. Amen.

EVERY DAY WITH JESUS

THOUGHT FOR TODAY

We can depend on the Bible, one day at a time.

WISDOM FROM SCRIPTURE

Because I love your commands more than gold,
 more than pure gold,
 and because I consider all your precepts right,
 I hate every wrong path.
Your statutes are wonderful; therefore I obey them.
The unfolding of your words gives light;
 it gives understanding to the simple.
I open my mouth and pant, longing for your commands.
Turn to me and have mercy on me,
 as you always do to those who love your name.
Direct my footsteps according to your word;
 let no sin rule over me.
Redeem me from the oppression of men,
 that I may obey your precepts.
Make your face shine upon your servant
 and teach me your decrees.
Your righteousness is everlasting and your law is true.
Trouble and distress have come upon me,
 but your commands are my delight.
Your statutes are forever right;
 give me understanding that I may live.
I call with all my heart; answer me, O Lord,
 and I will obey your decrees.
     —PSALMS 119:127-135, 142-145, NIV

I was attending a meeting of students in the state of Washington in the United States. We sat around a campfire and were having a wiener roast. We speared the frankfurters on pointed sticks and roasted them in the fire. The topic of our conversation was conversion.

A boy asked, "How do you bring yourself to the point of conversion? Just what do you do to bring it about? You talked as if it were such an easy thing to do to become a child of God."

I told the students about my experience, but one of them said, "I said yes to the Lord many years ago. What do you suppose is the reason I've regressed so much since then? I sometimes doubt I meant it seriously at the time."

A tall medical student answered him, "Once there was a boy who fell out of bed. His mother asked him how it happened and he answered, 'Mommy, it happened because I fell asleep too close to the place where I climbed in.'

"That is what happens to many Christians. When they are converted they think they have reached the goal. When one is converted and says yes to Jesus, it does not mean the end of a new experience, but the beginning of it. It is as if one entered a gate, the gate of conversion. To enter the kingdom of heaven through the gate of conversion means to enter into a world of riches. All the promises of the Bible become your property. But you have to find your way around in that world of riches. You have to find out what it means, 'For all the promises of God in Him are yea, and in Him Amen' (2 Corinthians 1:20, KJV). You have to find out how rich you are. If you think conversion means you have arrived at the end of the pathway in your life, you will fall out, for you fell asleep too close to the place where you climbed in."

Then I added, "At the moment of one's conversion he is

registered in heaven as one who has earned all the rights and privileges that make one a multi-millionaire in a spiritual sense. Ephesians 1:3 (KJV) says, 'He who hath blessed us with all spiritual blessings in heavenly places in Christ.'

"The Bible is a check book. When you said yes to Jesus Christ, many promises were deposited to your credit at that very moment, and they were signed by the Lord Jesus. But now you have to cash your checks to profit by them. When you come upon such a promise and say, 'Thank You, Lord, I accept this,' then you have cashed a check, and that day you'll be richer than you were the day before."

"Let's sing," a student suggested. The mountains echoed the song, "Every Day with Jesus Is Better Than the Day Before." One student remarked, "That's really true, at least if you cash no less than one check a day."

—*Amazing Love*

QUESTIONS TO CONSIDER
1. How will you learn to trust the Bible one day at a time?
2. What "check" do you need to cash with God today?

A PRAYERFUL RESPONSE
Lord, I will trust Your Word for my needs today. Amen.

A FIRM FOUNDATION

THOUGHT FOR TODAY

God's Word is a firm foundation when Satan challenges our faith.

WISDOM FROM SCRIPTURE

Be self-controlled and alert. Your enemy the devil prowls around like a roaring lion looking for someone to devour.

Resist him, standing firm in the faith, because you know that your brothers throughout the world are undergoing the same kind of sufferings.

And the God of all grace, who called you to his eternal glory in Christ, after you have suffered a little while, will himself restore you and make you strong, firm and steadfast.

Finally, be strong in the Lord and in his mighty power. Put on the full armor of God so that you can take your stand against the devil's schemes.

For our struggle is not against flesh and blood, but against the rulers, against the authorities, against the powers of this dark world and against the spiritual forces of evil in the heavenly realms.

Therefore put on the full armor of God, so that when the day of evil comes, you may be able to stand your ground, and after you have done everything, to stand.

Stand firm then, with the belt of truth buckled around your waist, with the breastplate of righteousness in place, and with your feet fitted with the readiness that comes from the gospel of peace.

In addition to all this, take up the shield of faith, with which you can extinguish all the flaming arrows of the evil one.

Take the helmet of salvation and the sword of the Spirit, which is the word of God.

—1 PETER 5:8-10; EPHESIANS 6:10-17, NIV

INSIGHTS FROM CORRIE TEN BOOM

With a kangaroo hop back to New Zealand for a return visit of two months before setting out for India, I was able to meet again many who had trusted the Lord for salvation. Faithfully they were studying a course in Scripture memorization.

Rarely am I able to revisit a country so soon—often it is five years—so what a delight to find the recently converted Christians had profited from this course, and not only they, but some of the older ones, too.

In Hamilton there was a family in which every member was faithfully studying the correspondence course, even Grandma. When the lessons were returned the youngest girl would ask, "Grandma, how many mistakes did you make? I only made two!" Seldom have I seen a family where every member had a practical knowledge of the Scriptures.

It is good to be certain why we find power in the Word of God. I have five reasons why I believe the Bible is inspired.

1. It says so! "Holy men of God spake as they were moved by the Holy Ghost" (2 Peter 1:21, KJV).

2. The effect it has upon all who believe and follow it.

3. Some of it was written more than two thousand years before the New Testament, yet the writers agree.

4. The authors do not offer any excuses for their own faults or sins.

5. The writers record some most harrowing scenes which affected them greatly, yet they never express one word of emotion. The Holy Spirit wanted the facts recorded, and not their feelings about the facts.

Many persons make the mistake to think they can measure the certainty of their salvation by their feelings. It is the Word of God that is their foundation and therefore it is essential to have a practical knowledge of the Bible. We need knowledge of the Sword of the Spirit. As the Lord Jesus used this Sword to overcome the evil one in temptation, so we must learn to defend ourselves against every sort of attack.

One of his favorite darts is, "It is not true that you are really saved." This must be met with Scripture such as 1 John 5:11-12 (KJV): "And this is the record, that God hath given to us eternal life, and this life is in his Son. He that hath the Son hath life; and he that hath not the Son of God hath not life."

Another form of attack is bringing to memory the weaknesses and sins of the past and suggesting we can never be a faithful follower of Christ. No amount of reasoning or argument can overcome this temptation but only the Word of God, which says in 1 Corinthians 10:13 (KJV), "There hath no temptation taken you but such as is common to man: but God is faithful, who will not suffer you to be tempted above that ye are able; but will with the temptation also make a way to escape, that ye may be able to bear it."

We must know the promises.

—*Plenty for Everyone*

QUESTIONS TO CONSIDER

1. How can you build a firm scriptural foundation for your faith?
2. What verse could you claim to ward off spiritual attacks?

A PRAYERFUL RESPONSE

Lord, I will learn Your promises so I can withstand the devil. Amen.

ABIDE AND BEAR FRUIT

THOUGHT FOR TODAY

When we abide in God's Word, we bear spiritual fruit.

WISDOM FROM SCRIPTURE

I am the true vine, and my Father is the vinegrower.

He removes every branch in me that bears no fruit. Every branch that bears fruit he prunes to make it bear more fruit.

You have already been cleansed by the word that I have spoken to you.

Abide in me as I abide in you. Just as the branch cannot bear fruit by itself unless it abides in the vine, neither can you unless you abide in me.

I am the vine, you are the branches. Those who abide in me and I in them bear much fruit, because apart from me you can do nothing.

Whoever does not abide in me is thrown away like a branch and withers; such branches are gathered, thrown into the fire, and burned.

If you abide in me, and my words abide in you, ask for whatever you wish, and it will be done for you.

My Father is glorified by this, that you bear much fruit and become my disciples.

—JOHN 15:1-8, NRSV

INSIGHTS FROM CORRIE TEN BOOM

Leaving New Zealand full of new zeal, I arrived in the state of Kerala, India, where I was to speak in a series of small conferences far back in the jungle.

My Indian companion met me at the airport and took me to a small place on the river where a canoe was waiting. We climbed in and started our trip down the peaceful river. Slowly our little craft glided over the shallow waters. Except for the rhythmic sound of the paddle and the occasional murmur of the soft wind in the trees, there was nothing to be heard.

My companion was the leader of a home group. Twice a year the home groups in the area came together in a conference to read the Bible, pray, and plead for revival. I was to speak three times a day in several such conferences which would be held in a *pandal*—a wide roof protecting the congregation from the hot sun. There are no walls so the breeze may pass through and the people sit on the grassy floor.

As the coolie paddled our canoe down the river, my Indian companion told me of the great longing in his heart to win souls for Jesus Christ.

"Yet I am not successful," he said. "I always give my testimony, but I am not able to persuade people to make a decision."

"Do you use the Sword of the Spirit, the Word of God?" I asked him.

"I fear I am not very adept at handling that Sword," he admitted. "Just at the critical moment I am never able to find a text that fits the situation."

"Yes, I can understand that," I confessed. "I sometimes have the same problem. However, I am now memorizing certain verses of Scripture which I call my first-aid course. These are emergency Scriptures I apply to the wound until I can look up the rest of the Scriptures, which will bring further healing."

My Indian companion brightened and then I told him of a recent experience in Canada where I had learned that it was not me, but the Word of God coming through me, that won people to Christ anyway. I turned and looked at my Indian friend. He was nodding his head in understanding.

"If we diligently read the Bible, the Holy Spirit will give us the right words and Scripture references," I said. "If we depend on Him, we are like the branches of these vines along the river which bear fruit. However, if the branches are broken off, then no fruit will appear."

By this time the forest had thinned out on either side of the river. We could see narrow paths which permitted the people to tread single file through the trees. It was almost dark and I saw, coming down the paths, files of Indian people carrying torches of lighted palm leaves in their hands. The white clothes they wore gave the scene a strange, ethereal appearance as though they were pilgrims walking to heaven. Many had gathered already in the *pandal* away in the distance and were singing a gospel song in a monotone, chanting it over and over as the white-robed pilgrims made their way to the meeting place.

After the meeting that night I lay in my little thatched hut, praising God for the power of the Word which had not only drawn these people together, but which had won them to the Lord Jesus Christ.

—Tramp for the Lord

QUESTIONS TO CONSIDER

1. When could you spend extended time abiding in God's Word?
2. As a result of abiding, what spiritual fruit would you like to bear?

A PRAYERFUL RESPONSE

Lord, teach me to abide in Your Word so I can bear spiritual fruit. Amen.

PART TWO

THE POWER OF PRAYER

There was a constant procession through this little back room.
Sometimes it was a customer; most often it was a visitor—
    all bringing their problems to Father.
Quite unabashedly, in the sight of customers in the front room
    and the employees working with us,
he would bow his head and pray for the answer.
He prayed over the work, too.
There weren't many repair problems he hadn't encountered.
But occasionally one would come along that baffled even him.
And then I would hear him say, "Lord, You know what
makes the planets spin and You know what makes this watch
    run...."
The answers to these prayers seemed often to come in the middle
    of the night:
many mornings I would climb onto my stool to find the watch
that we had left in a hundred despairing pieces
fitted together and ticking merrily.

THE HIDING PLACE

CORRIE TEN BOOM'S INSIGHT
We can apply the power of prayer to all aspects of life.

DAY 6

A RECIPE FOR PRAYER

THOUGHT FOR TODAY
Prayer joins together God's promises and our faith.

WISDOM FROM SCRIPTURE
He was praying in a certain place, and after he had finished, one of his disciples said to him, "Lord, teach us to pray, as John taught his disciples."

He said to them, "When you pray, say:
'Father, hallowed be your name.
Your kingdom come.
Give us each day our daily bread.
And forgive us our sins,
for we ourselves forgive everyone indebted to us.
And do not bring us to the time of trial.'"

And he said to them, "Suppose one of you has a friend, and you go to him at midnight and say to him, 'Friend, lend me three loaves of bread; for a friend of mine has arrived, and I have nothing to set before him.'

"And he answers from within, 'Do not bother me; the door has already been locked, and my children are with me in bed; I cannot get up and give you anything.'

"I tell you, even though he will not get up and give him anything because he is his friend, at least because of his persistence he will get up and give him whatever he needs.

"So I say to you, Ask, and it will be given you; search, and you will find; knock, and the door will be opened for you.

"For everyone who asks receives, and everyone who

searches finds, and for everyone who knocks, the door will be opened." LUKE 11:1-10, NRSV

INSIGHTS FROM CORRIE TEN BOOM

In the cell of a prison a woman lies on her cot with a bored expression on her face. She has a cheap novel in her hand, but it does not interest her much. Her needlework lies neglected on her chair. It is warm and it is Sunday.

I am visiting the cells after the sermon—an unusual privilege. Although I am allowed to speak at the meetings in prisons, the follow-up work is usually left to the regular prison evangelists. I sit near the Dutchwoman, and for a short time can share her life in the small cell—colorless, monotonous, without any view. I know what it is like from my own experience. I feel such great love and compassion for this woman, and pray that the Lord will give me entrance to her heart.

The ice is broken sooner than I expect, and we have a heart-to-heart talk. To begin with, the conversation is about baking cakes—a typical reaction engendered by the hunger which results from a monotonous diet. Carefully I try to turn our talk to deeper things. I discover that she has quite a good knowledge of the Bible, and it is easy to speak to her about eternal truths. She knows that Jesus died for her on the cross, but she is a backslider.

"Do you sometimes make use of the time that you are alone to pray?" I ask.

"I don't know how to pray," she says. "Tell me something of your prayer life."

"For cakes you need ingredients, and you need them for prayer, too. For instance, the ingredients of a prayer could be: 1) the promises of God, 2) our problems and needs, and 3) faith to bring these two together. If you don't understand me, I'll give you an example.

"Yesterday I was in darkness—really depressed. I didn't know what to do. When this happens I quietly spend a few minutes trying to find the reason. I asked God to show me the reason for the darkness. God will give His children a clear answer when they are willing to listen in obedience. It is a question of making use of the quiet time...."

The prisoner says, "When you talk like this, I really start to long to live the Christian life again. I am going to do my best."

I look smilingly at her. "Do you see this stick? Do you think it is possible for it to stand upright on its own? Of course not, for it is not the nature of the stick to stand by itself. It can do so only when my hand keeps it steady. It is not the nature of human beings to be able to stand on their own, either. They can do it only when they surrender to the hand that will keep them from falling. Look, here in Jude, verse 24, it is written, 'Now to Him who is able to keep you from falling and to present you before His glory without fault and with unspeakable joy'" (Phillips).

For a moment we are quiet together and I know that the Holy Spirit works in her heart. Then she surrenders to the hand that was wounded to save her.

—*Not Good If Detached*

Questions to Consider

1. What needs and worries will you bring to God today?
2. How can Corrie's recipe for prayer apply to these problems?

A Prayerful Response

Lord, I believe You will hear and answer my prayer. Amen.

UNEXPECTED BLESSINGS

THOUGHT FOR TODAY

When we pray for others, God blesses us, too.

WISDOM FROM SCRIPTURE

You have heard that it was said, "You shall love your neighbor and hate your enemy."

But I say to you, Love your enemies and pray for those who persecute you, so that you may be children of your Father in heaven; for he makes his sun rise on the evil and on the good, and sends rain on the righteous and on the unrighteous.

Ask, and it will be given you; search, and you will find; knock, and the door will be opened for you.

For everyone who asks receives, and everyone who searches finds, and for everyone who knocks, the door will be opened.

Is there anyone among you who, if your child asks for bread, will give a stone?

Or if the child asks for a fish, will give a snake?

If you then, who are evil, know how to give good gifts to your children, how much more will your Father in heaven give good things to those who ask him!

In everything do to others as you would have them do to you; for this is the law and the prophets.

—MATTHEW 5:43-45; 7:7-12, NRSV

INSIGHTS FROM CORRIE TEN BOOM

I once traveled by car through the mountains of California from Los Angeles to San Francisco. It is one of my weak points that I am afraid of driving through mountains with Americans. They usually drive at such great speed. Along one side of the road was a deep chasm and there were many dangerous curves.

I knew from experience what to do when the demon of fear entered my heart. He had called on me many times during my imprisonment in Germany, and I would then begin to sing. Singing always helps. Try it yourself some time; fear and anxiety will vanish when you sing.

So I sang one hymn after another, until my host, the driver, asked teasingly, "Are you afraid?"

"Yes," I said, "that is why I am singing."

But this time it was to no avail. Every time we approached a curve, I would think, *If another car is coming toward us from beyond that curve, we shall certainly crash into each other!* And, thoroughly frightened, I would stop singing.

No, singing did not help me. Then I tried to dispel my fear by prayer, and I prayed. But my prayer became a refrain: *Lord, bring us safely to San Francisco. Do not let us crash down into this abyss. Please grant that there will be no car approaching us from around that curve ahead.*

I kept on praying to dispel my fear until suddenly, and I do not know how the idea came to me, I began to pray for others. I prayed for everyone who came into my thoughts, people with whom I had traveled, those who had been in prison with me, my school friends of years ago. I do not know how long I continued in prayer, but this I do know: all fear was gone. Interceding for others had released me.

Some time ago in San Diego I met a man who told a story of the power of intercessory prayer. He had been a heavy drinker and was finally taken to a psychiatric hospital. He was placed in a room with three other patients who did nothing but scream. When night came he was in despair. He prayed, but could not fall asleep while the screams continued. Then suddenly he began to pray for the three patients, and just as suddenly the screams ceased.

"Not only that," continued the man, "it seemed as if something broke in me. When I prayed for others, my own tension was released and I was free. The next day I had to undergo a psychiatric examination. At its conclusion the doctor said, 'There is nothing wrong with you: you are normal.' I knew that night that I had become a free man."

Intercession often adds to its many other blessings the healing of one's own tension.

—Amazing Love

QUESTIONS TO CONSIDER
1. Have you ever experienced the relief of your own fear or tension while praying for others? If so, when?
2. For whom can you intercede? What, specifically, can you pray for the people in your life?

A PRAYERFUL RESPONSE
Lord, thank You for the unexpected blessings of intercession. Amen.

PRAY FOR THE HARVEST

THOUGHT FOR TODAY

If you want to work with God, learn to pray.

WISDOM FROM SCRIPTURE

When he saw the crowds, he had compassion for them, because they were harassed and helpless, like sheep without a shepherd.

Then he said to his disciples, "The harvest is plentiful, but the laborers are few;

therefore ask the Lord of the harvest to send out laborers into his harvest.

"Truly I tell you, whatever you bind on earth will be bound in heaven, and whatever you loose on earth will be loosed in heaven.

"Again, truly I tell you, if two of you agree on earth about anything you ask, it will be done for you by my Father in heaven.

"For where two or three are gathered in my name, I am there among them."

Pray without ceasing.

"And whenever you pray [alone], do not be like the hypocrites for they love to stand and pray in the synagogues and at the street corners so that they may be seen by others. Truly I tell you, they have received their reward.

But whenever you pray, go into your room and shut the door and pray to your Father who is in secret; and your Father who sees in secret will reward you."

—MATTHEW 9:36-38; 18:18-20; 1 THESSALONIANS 5:17;
MATTHEW 6:5-6, NRSV

During my trip from Formosa [now Taiwan] to Australia, I stay for five days in Hong Kong. This beautiful island has riches and poverty side by side. It has the most beautiful window displays in the world, but also many slums full of refugees. It is a piece of free China with huge problems.

My time there is full of activity. I am in contact with many consecrated Christians. The meetings are extremely well organized, every minute of the day put to good use.

One evening the Holy Spirit is obviously working in a group of young Christians who some time ago accepted Jesus Christ as their Savior. On this particular evening they come to a full surrender and accept Him as their Victor. "Thanks be to God, which giveth us the victory through our Lord Jesus Christ" (1 Corinthians 15:57, KJV).

One asks, "What is expected of us now?"

"The Lord will show you. Wait patiently for His guidance. But there is one thing I can advise you to do now, and that is to organize prayer cells. Prayer is not a prefix or a suffix; it is central. Over the whole world I see God gives His children prayer cells. It is not only the Communists who form cells, but wherever two or three come together in Jesus' name, there is a cell for Him. In eternity we shall see how important prayer meetings have been."

A group of students in Chicago prayed every week for a number of unsaved fellow students. Eventually everyone on the list was saved. One of them was Dr. Torrey Johnson, the founder of Youth for Christ. Wherever I have traveled over the world I have seen how this work has been blessed. Thousands of ten thousands have found their Savior through it.

What was the first cause? Torrey Johnson? No, the prayers of those young men in Chicago. Intercession is so tremendously important that in Isaiah 59:16 (KJV) it is written, "[God] wondered that there was no intercessor."

If you will work *for* God, form a committee. If you will work *with* God, form a prayer group.

That evening we make plans for a weekly prayer meeting and later I hear that more have commenced. The greatest thing we can do for one another is to pray. Prayer is striking the winning blow at the concealed enemy; our service is gathering up the results.

—Not Good If Detached

QUESTIONS TO CONSIDER
1. How can you begin praying for God's spiritual harvest?
2. Who could join you as you pray?

A PRAYERFUL RESPONSE
Lord, please bring more workers into the spiritual harvest, including me. Amen.

DAY 9

THE KEY FOR THE DAY

THOUGHT FOR TODAY
Prayer is the key for the day, the lock for the night.

WISDOM FROM SCRIPTURE
It is good to give thanks to the Lord,
to sing praises to your name, O Most High;
to declare your steadfast love in the morning,
and your faithfulness by night,
to the music of the lute and the harp,
to the melody of the lyre.
For you, O LORD, have made me glad by your work;
at the works of your hands I sing for joy.
How great are your works, O LORD!
Your thoughts are very deep!
The dullard cannot know,
the stupid cannot understand this:
though the wicked sprout like grass
and all evildoers flourish,
they are doomed to destruction forever,
but you, O LORD, are on high forever.
For your enemies, O Lord,
for your enemies shall perish;
all evildoers shall be scattered.
But you have exalted my horn like that of the wild ox;
you have poured over me fresh oil.
My eyes have seen the downfall of my enemies;
my ears have heard the doom of my evil assailants.
The righteous flourish like the palm tree,
and grow like a cedar in Lebanon.

They are planted in the house of the LORD;
    they flourish in the courts of our God.
In old age they still produce fruit;
    they are always green and full of sap,
showing that the LORD is upright;
he is my rock, and there is no unrighteousness in him.
                      —PSALM 92, NRSV

INSIGHTS FROM CORRIE TEN BOOM

One evening in Honolulu the conversation is about prayer. Lailani says, "I think it is very difficult to pray."

"No wonder," I reply. "Even the disciples did not find it easy. They asked the Lord to teach them how to pray. It is a strategic point. The devil smiles when we are up to our ears in work, but he trembles when we pray. Sometimes I think there must be a map of the world both in heaven and hell. The most important points are not the Kremlin in Moscow, or the Pentagon building in Washington, but the places where two or three are gathered in Jesus' name in prayer meetings."

When the Americans entered Germany after the war, a law was made forbidding fraternization. In one minister's family were two teenage children. At school they had heard terrible things about the Americans. One day the girls saw an American officer coming toward their house, and cried, "Look, Father, he is coming to our house."

"Don't be afraid. Americans are not barbarians."

The officer entered the house and when he came into their room, said, "We are forbidden to speak and eat together, but nobody has forbidden us to pray together."

He knelt down and the minister and his family followed. Into the hearts of the children at that moment came a great love for the Americans. Prayer is like Jacob's ladder. Angels go up and down, but it is God who places the ladder.

"But I find I have no time to pray," says Lailani.

"You remind me of a German minister with far too big a congregation who said he was really too busy to pray. He had plenty of theology, but no 'kneeology.' That is just as fruitless as a beautiful lamp without electricity.

"My full schedule and constant traveling from one place to another can sometimes bring me into the same danger. In the morning I must awaken early to travel; in the evening I roll into bed dead tired. But we must begin each day by tuning our instruments with the help of the great Conductor. Prayer is the key for the day, the lock for the night. When Satan cannot keep us from doing the work for the Lord he comes behind us and pushes us into doing too much work, and much we do is not right."

After our conversation we sing with a group:

Drop Thy still dews of quietness,
Till all our strivings cease;
Take from our souls the strain and stress,
And let our ordered lives confess
The beauty of Thy peace.

Lailani sings with us, and I know that her heart prays.

—*Not Good If Detached*

QUESTIONS TO CONSIDER
1. What do you find difficult about prayer?
2. How can you move past this difficulty?

A PRAYERFUL RESPONSE
Lord, remind me to begin and end each day with prayer. Amen.

Pray About Everything

Thought for Today
God cares about and wants to hear all of our requests.

Wisdom from Scripture
But whenever you pray, go into your room and shut the door and pray to your Father who is in secret; and your Father who sees in secret will reward you.

When you are praying, do not heap up empty phrases as the Gentiles do; for they think that they will be heard because of their many words.

Do not be like them, for your Father knows what you need before you ask him.

Rejoice in the Lord always, again I will say, Rejoice.

Let your gentleness be known to everyone. The Lord is near.

Do not worry about anything, but in everything by prayer and supplication, with thanksgiving let your requests be made known to God.

And the peace of God, which surpasses all understanding, will guard your hearts and your minds in Christ Jesus.

Finally, beloved, whatever is true, whatever is honorable, whatever is just, whatever is pure, whatever is pleasing, whatever is commendable, if there is any excellence and if there is anything worthy of praise, think about these things.

—Matthew 6:6-8; Philippians 4:4-8, NRSV

At a meeting I have spoken about answered prayer. The evening is warm, and before we go to bed we sit outside and talk.

A young immigrant asks, "Can you really trouble God with the petty things of your life? I dare to speak with God about my soul, but I carry the sorrows of every day alone."

I answered, "Have you ever thought what God's love for us means? Love demands love, and don't you think that we can make God's father-heart happy by showing Him our love in telling Him of our cares? Earthly parents are happy when their children expect much from them. In Psalms 147:11 it says, 'The Lord taketh pleasure in those that hope in His mercy.' Don't forget that God sees our sorrows through our eyes.

"Imagine a little girl who comes crying to her mother because her doll is broken. Her mother doesn't say, 'Come along, don't be silly; that doll isn't worth a penny. What nonsense to cry about it.' No, she understands perfectly that the doll is the little one's sweetheart, and she tries to comfort her and says, 'Let us look and see if we can mend the doll.' Because she loves, she sees the catastrophe through the eyes of the child. God loves us more than an earthly father or mother. And His love makes our problems great in His eyes and small in our eyes.

"I will tell you something that happened when I was a prisoner in a concentration camp with my sister, Betsie. One morning I had a terrible cold and I said to Betsie, 'What can O do? I have no handkerchief.'

"'Pray,' she said. I smiled, but she prayed, 'Father, Corrie has got a cold, and she has no handkerchief. Will You give her one? In Jesus' name, Amen.' I could not help but laugh, but as she said 'Amen' I heard my name called. I went to the window, and there stood my friend who worked in the prison hospital.

"'Quickly, quickly! Take this little package,' and inside was a handkerchief.

"'Why in the world did you bring me this? Did I ask you for it? Did you know that I have a cold?'

"'No, but I was folding handkerchiefs in the hospital, and a voice in my heart said, *Take one to Corrie ten Boom.*'

"What a miracle! Can you understand what that handkerchief told me at that moment? It told me that in heaven there is a loving Father who hears when one of His children asks for an impossible little thing—a handkerchief. And that heavenly Father tells one of His other children to take one to Corrie ten Boom. We cannot understand, but the foolishness of God is so much higher than the wisdom of the wise. God's proportions are so different from ours.

"Perhaps in His eyes New Zealand is just as unimportant as a handkerchief. Perhaps in His eyes a handkerchief is just as important as New Zealand. I don't know. But this I do know: God answers prayers, and God's promises are a greater reality than our problems."

—*Not Good If Detached*

QUESTIONS TO CONSIDER

1. What do you think is too petty to pray about? Why?
2. Think of a time when God answered a "small" request. What did that teach you about Him?

A PRAYERFUL RESPONSE

Lord, I will pray about everything in my life, not just the "big" things. Amen.

Breaking Down Resistance

Thought for Today

Prayer can penetrate hard hearts with God's love.

Wisdom from Scripture

Therefore, as the Holy Spirit says,

"Today, if you hear his voice,

do not harden your hearts as in the rebellion,

as on the day of testing in the wilderness,

where your ancestors put me to the test,

though they had seen my works for forty years...."

Take care, brothers and sisters, that none of you may have an evil, unbelieving heart that turns away from the living God.

But exhort one another every day, as long as it is called "today," so that none of you may be hardened by the deceitfulness of sin.

For we have become partners of Christ, if only we hold our first confidence firm to the end.

Since, then, we have a great high priest who has passed through the heavens, Jesus, the Son of God, let us hold fast to our confession.

For we do not have a high priest who is unable to sympathize with our weaknesses, but we have one who in every respect has been tested as we are, yet without sin.

Let us therefore approach the throne of grace with boldness, so that we may receive mercy and find grace to help in time of need.

—Hebrews 3:7-10, 12-14; 4:14-16, NRSV

"How can I bring my husband to the Lord?" a lady asked me. She was a true child of God, but she did not yet know there were dozens of promises in the Bible.

"When I am in the same room with him," she continued, "it is sometimes as though a cloud of darkness overshadows me."

"Act God's love," I told her. "In Romans 5:5 it is written, 'The love of God is shed abroad in our hearts by the Holy Ghost which is given unto us.' There are two kinds of love—human love and God's love. Human love fails; God's love never fails. When you are alone with your husband and feel that his depression touches you, pray this prayer: 'Thank you, Lord Jesus, that God's love has been put into my heart through the Holy Spirit who is given to me, and thank You, Father, that Your love in me is victorious over this darkness.'"

Later on we met again and she said, "The Lord is working. My husband is so much happier and less depressed. I often repeat the prayer that you gave me and I know that if I give room to the Holy Spirit, then I become a channel for His love, which is the fruit of the Spirit."

It was also at this church that I spoke to a group of young people about surrender. Looking around the meeting, I could see two girls were resisting the Holy Spirit as their faces grew harder and harder.

I prayed to the Lord for wisdom and guidance. In obeying Him, I paused in my message and said, "Young people, there are two among you who are resisting the Holy Spirit. If they continue there is a danger they will go home poorer than they were when they came in. But if they stop resisting they will go home richer. For the Lord has a blessing for them. Let us pray together that the Lord will send away the spirit of disobedience and break their resistance by the Holy Spirit."

I believe that sometimes it is better, even necessary, to take the offensive. We are able to do this knowing that we stand on the victorious side, overcoming by the blood of the Lamb (see Revelation 12:11).

After praying I went on with my talk, refraining from looking at the two girls. At the close of the meeting one of them asked how I had known she had rejected the Lord. I replied that both her face and the Holy Spirit had shown it clearly.

She continued, "It is true. I have a boyfriend who is not a Christian and I was so afraid I would have to give him up, I was not willing to surrender. But now I see that I must."

I asked, "Will you pray, 'Lord Jesus, make me willing to be made willing to surrender all?'"

She did, and I saw something of the unspeakable joy, full of glory, on her face. To lose your life for Jesus' sake is to win it. What a joy that is!

Prayer had broken the resistance! As someone has pointed out, the sermon which brought three thousand souls to Christ and from which the missionary movement from Jerusalem was launched, began as ten days of prayer in an upper room.

—Plenty for Everyone

QUESTIONS TO CONSIDER

1. What resistance, either yours or others, affects your walk with God?
2. What specific prayer can you form to dissolve this resistance?

A PRAYERFUL RESPONSE

Lord, teach me to pray in a way that breaks spiritual resistance. Amen.

CONFESS AND BE FREE

THOUGHT FOR TODAY
Confession frees us to receive from God.

WISDOM FROM SCRIPTURE
This is the message we have heard from him and proclaim to you, that God is light and in him there is no darkness at all.

If we say that we have fellowship with him while we are walking in darkness, we lie and do not do what is true; but if we walk in the light as he himself is in the light, we have fellowship with one another, and the blood of Jesus his Son cleanses us from all sin.

If we say that we have no sin, we deceive ourselves, and the truth is not in us.

If we confess our sins, he who is faithful and just will forgive us our sins and cleanse us from all unrighteousness.

If we say that we have not sinned, we make him a liar, and his word is not in us.

My little children, I am writing these things to you so that you may not sin. But if anyone does sin, we have an advocate with the Father, Jesus Christ the righteous; and he is the atoning sacrifice for our sins, and not for ours only but also for the sins of the whole world.

Now by this we may be sure that we know him, if we obey his commandments.

Whoever says, "I have come to know him," but does not obey his commandments, is a liar, and in such a person the truth does not exist; but whoever obeys his word, truly in this person the love of God has reached perfection.

By this we may be sure that we are in him: whoever says, "I abide in him," ought to walk just as he walked.

—1 JOHN 1:5-2:6, NRSV

INSIGHTS FROM CORRIE TEN BOOM

In England two ladies came to me after a meeting: they were neighbors. One had been praying for the other for several weeks. It was easy to see that the other needed prayer, for her eyes were sad. And so I prayed with them that God would give us a profitable talk with understanding on both sides.

Then I asked her, "Have you ever received Jesus as your Savior?"

"No, I haven't, but I would like to."

I showed her how Jesus in His great love asks us to make a decision to trust Him. He holds out the great gift of salvation, but we must be willing to stretch out our hands to take it.

"I wish I could...," she replied wistfully.

"Why not?"

"I don't know, but really my heart longs to have peace. I know Jesus is willing and able to give me peace and salvation, but it is as if something is holding me back. I have often heard the gospel, but something is holding me back."

"When did you go to a fortune teller?" I asked.

Looking a little surprised she told me she had been to one the year before.

"But what has that to do with the things we are talking about now?" she asked. "I did it for fun and don't really believe in fortune tellers."

"Do you realize that you have sinned in God's eyes? God calls this an abomination, and that is the reason you cannot accept the Lord."

I opened my Bible and read Deuteronomy 18:10-13 (KJV): "There shall not be found among you any one that ... useth divination, or an observer of times, or an enchanter, or a witch, or a charmer, or a consulter with familiar spirits, or a wizard, or a necromancer. For all that do these things are an abomination unto the LORD: and because of these abominations the LORD thy God doth drive them out from before thee. Thou shalt be perfect with the LORD thy God."

I told her, "These things are an abomination in God's eyes and if we have anything to do with them, it means we are seeking help from the enemy instead of from God."

"I did not know this was a sin but I see it now," she said.

"I am glad you do. Now listen to what the Bible says in 1 John 1:7 and 9. It tells us to confess and be cleansed. The blood of Jesus cleanses you from all the sins you confess."

I prayed with her and thanked God for His warning and forgiveness shown in His Word; and she did what I told her to do. Her prayer was like the cry of one longing to be saved.

"Oh Lord, forgive me for this sin in Jesus' name. I did not know it was such a great sin. I thought it was only foolishness but I see now. Forgive me and make me free."

Again I showed her the way of salvation, and without any hesitation she said, "Lord Jesus, I receive You as my Savior."

—Plenty for Everyone

QUESTIONS TO CONSIDER

1. To be spiritually free, what do you need to confess to God?
2. Are you willing to confess your sins and be forgiven now? Why, or why not?

A PRAYERFUL RESPONSE

Lord, I want to confess my sins to You and be spiritually free. Amen.

PART THREE

THE JOY OF OBEDIENCE

The hunted people kept coming, and the needs were often
more complicated than ration cards and addresses.
If a Jewish woman became pregnant, where could she go to
     have her baby?
If a Jew in hiding died, how could he be buried?
An uncanny realization had been growing in me.
We were friends with half of Haarlem!
We knew someone in every business and service in the city.
We didn't know, of course, the political views of all these people.
But—and here I felt a strange leaping of my heart—God did!
My job was simply to follow His leading one step at a time,
holding every decision up to Him in prayer.
I knew I was not clever or subtle or sophisticated;
if the Beje was becoming a meeting place for need and supply,
it was through some strategy far higher than mine.

THE HIDING PLACE

CORRIE TEN BOOM'S INSIGHT

If we obey, God will show us His way—and His way is
true joy.

DAY 13

NOT BY ACCIDENT

THOUGHT FOR TODAY
Obedience leads us to God's divine appointments.

WISDOM FROM SCRIPTURE
I guide you in the way of wisdom
and lead you along straight paths.
When you walk, your steps will not be hampered;
when you run, you will not stumble.
Hold on to instruction, do not let it go;
guard it well, for it is your life.
Do not set foot on the path of the wicked
or walk in the way of evil men.
Avoid it, do not travel on it;
turn from it and go on your way.
The path of the righteous is like the first gleam of dawn,
shining ever brighter till the full light of day.
But the way of the wicked is like deep darkness;
they do not know what makes them stumble.
My son, pay attention to what I say;
listen closely to my words.
Do not let them out of your sight,
keep them within your heart;
for they are life to those who find them
and health to a man's whole body.
Above all else, guard your heart,
for it is the wellspring of life.
—PROVERBS 4:11-15; 18-23, NIV

It is a wonderful life that is guided by a God who never makes mistakes. The only condition laid upon us is obedience.

"When are you going to bring this message to the Japanese?" a friend asks me after he hears one of my lectures. Until then I have worked only in America and Europe, Japan being far from my thoughts.

In my quiet time the instruction comes distinctly: *Go to Japan.*

I almost answer, "Yes, but…"

Obedience says, "Yes, Lord," and I have learned to obey. I want to say, "Yes, but I know nobody there; I can't speak the language and it is so expensive." Again and again, I begin counting and forget that my heavenly treasurer reckons differently from me.

The money comes, enough for a flight to Tokyo, where I arrive safely. It is raining, and from the air Tokyo looks dark and dreary. I am not at all sure of myself. In the customs office a man asks me where he is to take my suitcase. I tell him I do not know.

"Is someone going to meet you?"

"No, nobody," I answer.

In his own car he takes me to a hotel. It is small, dirty, and dark, but the manager understands some English. But now there is conflict in my soul. *Was that really God's guidance? What if it was a mistake?* I hardly dare go outdoors for fear I might lose my way back to the hotel. *Who would understand me?* It becomes a real temptation from Satan. How terribly God's children are tempted in these times.

Then I read in 1 Peter 1 that we are guarded by God's power until we fully enter into our spiritual heritage. The passage continues, "This means tremendous joy to you, I know, even though at present you are harassed by all kinds of trials and temptations. This is *no accident*—it happens to prove your faith, which is infinitely more valuable than gold, and gold as you know, even though it is ultimately perishable, must be purified by fire. This proving of your faith is *planned* to bring you praise and honor and glory in the day of Jesus Christ" (1 Pt 1:6-7, Phillips).

No accident—planned! God makes no mistakes! How it happens I cannot explain, but trust takes the place of doubt and I can say, "Lord, I know I am safe in Your everlasting arms. You are guiding me and will surely make the next step plain."

Then comes to mind: *David Morken.* Is that God's answer? Years ago I met David at a Youth for Christ meeting and he told me he might be sent to Japan. Fortunately the telephone directory is printed in English, and there is his name.

How wonderful, for the next step is clear. I pick up the telephone and hear a voice saying, "Mashie, mashie." In confusion I replace the receiver. I cannot even make a telephone call in this strange land of strange people speaking a strange language. Finally, the manager gets the number for me and I speak to David.

That day I am his guest, after which he secures a room for me in an InterVarsity Christian Fellowship house. The first week I speak three times, the second week eighteen times, and the third week twenty-six times. A season of unusual blessings awaits me.

How happy I am that I said "Yes, Lord," instead of "Yes, but..."

—*Not Good If Detached*

QUESTIONS TO CONSIDER
1. How has God been asking you to obey Him?
2. What has been your response to God?

A PRAYERFUL RESPONSE
Lord, I am willing to be made willing to obey You. Amen.

DAY 14

GETTING TO YES

THOUGHT FOR TODAY

To serve God, we must set aside barriers to our relationship with Him.

WISDOM FROM SCRIPTURE

"But if serving the Lord seems undesirable to you, then choose for yourselves this day whom you will serve, whether the gods your forefathers served beyond the River, or the gods of the Amorites, in whose land you are living. But as for me and my household, we will serve the Lord."

Then the people answered, "Far be it from us to forsake the Lord to serve other gods! It was the Lord our God himself who brought us and our fathers up out of Egypt, from that land of slavery, and performed those great signs before our eyes. He protected us on our entire journey and among all the nations through which we traveled. And the Lord drove out before us all the nations, including the Amorites, who lived in the land. We too will serve the Lord, because he is our God."

Then Joshua said, "You are witnesses against yourselves that you have chosen to serve the Lord."

Yes, we are witnesses," they replied.

"Now then," said Joshua, "throw away the foreign gods that are among you and yield your hearts to the Lord, the God of Israel."

And the people said to Joshua, "We will serve the Lord our God and obey him."

—JOSHUA 24:15-18; 22-24, NIV

Returning to Holland after my release from the German concentration camp at Ravensbruck, I said, "One thing I hope is that I'll never have to go back to Germany again. I am willing to go wherever God may want me to go, but I hope He'll never send me to Germany."

If we want to experience the guidance of God in our lives, we must accept one condition: obedience to Him.

On my trips to the United States I often spoke on the conditions in Europe during the postwar years, and when I talked of the chaos in Germany, people sometimes asked me, "Why don't you go to Germany, since you know the language?"

But I didn't want to go.

Then darkness came into my fellowship with God. When I asked for His guidance, there was no answer. God does not want us to be in doubt about His guidance, and I knew something had come between God and me. I prayed, "Lord, is there some disobedience in my life?"

The answer was very distinct: *Germany.*

I could see again the land I left in 1944. In my mind I could hear the harsh voices and my answer was long in coming. "Yes, Lord, I'll go to Germany, too. I'll follow wherever You lead."

Then when I returned to Holland from the United States, I learned that it was not yet possible for Hollanders to obtain a visa for visiting Germany. And I was glad.

I received an invitation to attend an international conference in Switzerland, and God told me I would meet some Germans there who would help me obtain a visa. Arriving at the conference I found representatives from many other countries, but not one German. And I was glad.

But on the last day of the conference there were two new arrivals. The instant they appeared, I could see they were Germans. I asked if they could help me with my papers, and one of the latecomers was director of the *Evangelisches Hilfswerk*, the church organization for the assistance of refugees.

"If we send you an invitation to come to Germany, you will be able to get your visa," he said. And so I went back to Germany.

Was it difficult? At times it was; at times it was not.

There is a sanctified Germany and a poisoned Germany. There is a Germany that has lost everything, where the hearts of people are a vacuum. Who is going to fill them? It is wonderful to speak there about Him who renews hearts and fills them with His joy.

Years ago I told the story of Jesus' feeding the five thousand with five loaves and two fishes to a class of boys. Carl had become so absorbed in the story that he jumped to his feet and shouted, "There is enough, there is enough, take as much as you want, there is enough!"

Dear little Carl, I wish more people were as much on fire about it as you.

—Amazing Love

Questions to Consider
1. Do you harbor a barrier to obeying God? If so, what is it?
2. How can you dismantle this barrier?

A Prayerful Response
Lord, I give You my barriers to serving and obeying You. Amen.

JOYFUL SURRENDER

THOUGHT FOR TODAY

Total surrender to God fills us with unexplainable joy.

WISDOM FROM SCRIPTURE

Do not store up for yourselves treasures on earth, where moth and rust destroy, and where thieves break in and steal.

But store up for yourselves treasures in heaven, where moth and rust do not destroy, and where thieves do not break in and steal.

For where your treasure is, there your heart will be also.

The eye is the lamp of the body. If your eyes are good, your whole body will be full of light.

But if your eyes are bad, your whole body will be full of darkness. If then the light within you is darkness, how great is that darkness!

No one can serve two masters. Either he will hate the one and love the other, or he will be devoted to the one and despise the other. You cannot serve both.

Do not be yoked together with unbelievers. For what do righteousness and wickedness have in common? Or what fellowship can light have with darkness?

What harmony is there between Christ and Belial? What does a believer have in common with an unbeliever?

What agreement is there between the temple of God and idols? For we are the temple of the living God. As God has said: "I will live with them and walk among them, and I will be their God, and they will be my people."

"Therefore come out from them and be separate, says

the Lord. Touch no unclean thing, and I will receive you.

"I will be a Father to you, and you will be my sons and daughters," says the Lord Almighty.

Since we have these promises, dear friends, let us purify ourselves from everything that contaminates body and spirit, perfecting holiness out of reverence for God.

MATTHEW 6:19-24; 2 CORINTHIANS 6:14-7:1, NIV

INSIGHTS FROM CORRIE TEN BOOM

Two girls come to me for advice and they tell me their difficulties.

One says, "I am a Christian. My parents are Buddhists. When they go to the temple to worship at the shrine they expect me to go with them. I do not believe in Buddha and I want to know if it is wrong for me to go with them without believing in what they say there. I go to make my parents happy and do not believe it can do me any harm."

I pray for wisdom and then tell her, "The Lord Jesus has bought you with His blood—a high price. He has a legal right to possess you wholly. You can never make a compromise with Him. He says, 'No man can serve two masters.' Do you lose something by accepting that? Yes, it means that for Jesus' sake you lose your life, but you win a far better life. Is it costly to accept? Yes, but it is far more costly to reject."

The other girl tells me of an almost greater conflict. "I am engaged to be married to a Buddhist," she explains. "He thinks it is all right for me to follow Jesus. He allows me to go to church and has promised when we are married he will give me complete freedom. What do you think of that?"

"The Bible says it is not possible to be unequally yoked with an unbeliever. Do you know what an unequal yoke is? Two animals of unequal strength put together to pull a cart are dragging against each other in an unequal yoke and that makes suffering for both. It is really an impossibility," I say. "The Lord Jesus makes Himself very clear in this. Those who will follow Him must belong to Him and follow Him in everything. He who loses His life for Jesus' sake has Him as Lord and King in every part of his life, and is, therefore, a yoke-fellow with Jesus. What riches! With Him we are more than conquerors."

After we have prayed together, both the girls surrender their whole lives into the hands of the Savior—an absolute surrender.

A month later I meet a sister of one of these girls in Hong Kong. She tells me, "Since their surrender both of the girls are intensely happy. Their letters are full of joy. One wrote to say that she told her fiancé she cannot marry him and there is now a great peace in her heart."

What is total surrender? A joyful experience.

—*Not Good If Detached*

QUESTIONS TO CONSIDER
1. What does total surrender mean to you?
2. In what area of your life do you need to surrender? How will you do this?

A PRAYERFUL RESPONSE
Lord, I cannot serve two masters. I surrender all to You. Amen.

LOOK UP AND FOLLOW

THOUGHT FOR TODAY

God asks us to look up and follow Him.

WISDOM FROM SCRIPTURE

From that time on Jesus began to preach, "Repent, for the kingdom of heaven is near."

As Jesus was walking beside the Sea of Galilee, he saw two brothers, Simon called Peter and his brother Andrew. They were casting a net into the lake, for they were fishermen.

"Come, follow me," Jesus said, "and I will make you fishers of men."

At once they left their nets and followed him.

Going on from there, he saw two other brothers, James son of Zebedee and his brother John. They were in a boat with their father Zebedee, preparing their nets. Jesus called them, and immediately they left the boat and their father and followed him.

Jesus went throughout Galilee, teaching in their synagogues, preaching the good news of the kingdom, and healing every disease and sickness among the people.

Therefore, since we are surrounded by such a great cloud of witnesses, let us throw off everything that hinders and the sin that so easily entangles, and let us run with perseverance the race marked out for us.

Let us fix our eyes on Jesus, the author and perfecter of our faith, who for the joy set before him endured the cross, scorning its shame, and sat down at the right hand of the throne of God. Consider him who endured such opposition from sinful men, so that you will not grow weary and lose heart.

—MATTHEW 4:17-23; HEBREWS 12:1-3, NIV

INSIGHTS FROM CORRIE TEN BOOM

A paratroop instructor said that there are four commands he gives his parachutists: *Attention! Stand in the door! Look up! Follow me!* Then the men have to jump.

Jesus is preparing men and women for the new heaven and the new earth and has given His co-workers the same orders the parachutists receive.

Attention! Some people do not believe that there are souls to be saved for eternity. They think everyone will be saved as a matter of course. They need to hear the bad news before the glad news has any value.

During the last war friends often warned me of the danger of working in the underground movement to save the Jewish people in Holland and told me of the cruel treatment which would befall me if I should be caught and sent to a concentration camp. To such warnings I always replied that these stories of such atrocities could not be true—that they must surely be anti-German propaganda—and so I turned a deaf ear to them.

But did my deaf ear help me when I was in Ravensbruck and saw my sister and thousands of other people perish at the hands of the Nazis? It did not help me at all. And neither will it help a person, when he is in hell, to have disbelieved in the existence of hell. If we love people we must tell them of the danger of a lost eternity.

Stand in the door! In my travels throughout the world I have often visited mission fields and what a joy it has been to be used by God for the strengthening of missionaries. But there are far more women than men in this work for the Lord. I think there must have been some young men who, when surrendering their lives to Jesus Christ, prayed, "Here I am, Lord, but do send my sister."

"Stand in the door" means that we must be obedient and go where God tells us, whether it be a call to the mission field or a call to work for Him at home. He can use us only when we are in the place where He wants us to be. We dare not keep the gospel a secret but must herald His story forth to all.

Look up! When we look at ourselves we feel unable to be used by the Lord, but when we look to Jesus we become His mirrors. It is true that by itself a mirror does not do much; but when it is hung or placed in the right position it does its job properly. It is very important, therefore, that we should be in the right position. And that position, for a Christian, is "looking unto Jesus the author and finisher of our faith" (Hebrews 12:2, KJV), for we have no light by ourselves.

Unfortunately, there are times in our lives when we experience a different truth:

"Mine iniquities have taken hold upon me (hindered me), so that I am not able to look up" (Psalms 40:12, KJV). On these occasions it is necessary to bring our sins in repentance to the Lord Jesus and restore our vision of Calvary.

Follow me! Denying ourselves, taking up our crosses and following Jesus is not like jumping from an airplane toward earth with parachutes on our backs. It means being safe in the hands of Jesus, yoke-bearers with Him. His joy in us and our joy fulfilled.

When we trust ourselves we are doing the wrong thing. We can fall into the error of spiritual pride on the one hand or discouragement on the other. We are really strong when we are weak; weak when we are strong. So following in the footsteps of Jesus, taking the steps—yes, and the jumps into the unknown—we can become paratroopers. We can storm the enemy's territory and win souls for Jesus. But only if we obey.

—*Plenty for Everyone*

QUESTIONS TO CONSIDER
1. Are you willing to follow God, not knowing the outcome? Why or why not?
2. What will it cost you to look up and follow Him?

A PRAYERFUL RESPONSE
Lord, I will fix my eyes on You and follow. Amen.

STRENGTH IN WEAKNESS

THOUGHT FOR TODAY
God will strengthen us so we can obey His instructions.

WISDOM FROM SCRIPTURE
But [God] said to me, "My grace is sufficient for you, for my power is made perfect in weakness." Therefore I will boast all the more gladly about my weaknesses, so that Christ's power may rest on me.

That is why, for Christ's sake, I delight in weaknesses, in insults, in hardships, in persecutions, in difficulties. For when I am weak, then I am strong.

For the foolishness of God is wiser than man's wisdom, and the weakness of God is stronger than man's strength.

Brothers, think of what you were when you were called. Not many of you were wise by human standards; not many were influential; not many were of noble birth.

But God chose the foolish things of the world to shame the wise; God chose the weak things of the world to shame the strong.

He chose the lowly things of this world and the despised things—and the things that are not—to nullify the things that are, so that no one may boast before him.

It is because of him that you are in Christ Jesus, who has become for us wisdom from God—that is, our righteousness, holiness, and redemption.

Therefore, as it is written: "Let him who boasts boast in the Lord."

2 CORINTHIANS 12:9-10; 1 CORINTHIANS 1:25-31, NIV

I was in Argentina. One day I was asked to visit some patients in a hospital. There had been a terrible polio epidemic. For the first time in my life I saw people lying in iron lungs. The tragedy so overcame me that I could hardly bear it.

A nurse asked me, "Will you speak with that Jewish man there?" He was not in an iron lung, but lay on a bed that went up and down. When his legs went up, his midriff pushed against his lungs and he could breathe out. When his legs went down, he could breathe in. He was fed by a little tube in his nose. He could not speak, but he could write.

When I looked at him I said in despair, "Oh Lord, I cannot do this. Please let me go somewhere else so I can cry in a corner. I am not able to speak to this man."

When I say to the Lord, "I cannot do this," I always receive the answer, *I have known that for a long time, but it is good that you know it too, for now you can let Me do it.* And I said, "Lord, then You do it." And He did. I spoke to this man.

I showed him an embroidery—that one side shows only a tangle of threads, but on the other a beautiful crown. I said, "When I see you lying on this bed I think of this embroidery. There has been a time in my life when it seemed like the tangled side of this crown. I saw no pattern, no beauty, no harmony. I was in prison, where my sister died before my eyes. But all that time I knew that God has no problems, only plans. There is never panic in heaven.

"Later on I saw God's side of the pattern. Because I had to go through deep suffering in that prison, I was able to comfort people afterward because I could tell them, 'Jesus is stronger than the deepest darkness. When you have experienced the darkness of a concentration camp, you know how deep that darkness can be!'"

Then I spoke to him about the Messiah, Jesus, the Son of God, who died on the cross for our sins. "It seemed when He died as if the whole plan of His life was broken, but there He answered the problem of sin for the whole world. He carried our punishment. And Jesus not only died for us, but He lives, for He is risen from the dead. He will even live in our hearts. We may use His name and pray in His name."

I told the man this happy message of Jesus' death and life. The man took a piece of paper and wrote, *I see already the beautiful side of the embroidery of my life.*

What a victory it was for him to lie there, not being able to move or speak or breathe, and in spite of all this, to see God's side. That was a great miracle. We had a good time together and I was so thankful. I could pray and then thank the Lord with him.

The next day I went again to the hospital and asked the nurse, "May I speak with him again?" She told me that he had beckoned her when I left and then wrote on his little writing pad: *For the first time in my life I have prayed in Jesus' name.* Then he closed his eyes and died.

This Jewish man found Jesus in the last moment of his life. And God used me when I was not able to do it. Yes, God's strength is demonstrated in our weakness.

—*Marching Orders for the End Battle*

Questions to Consider
1. What weakness keeps you from serving God faithfully?
2. How could God turn your weakness into strength?

A Prayerful Response
Lord, thank You that when I am weak, You are strong. Amen.

TRUSTING GOD

THOUGHT FOR TODAY

God asks us to trust Him for our provisions.

WISDOM FROM SCRIPTURE

And my God will meet all your needs according to his glorious riches in Christ Jesus.

Therefore I tell you, do not worry about your life, what you will eat or what you will drink; or about your body, what you will wear. Is not life more important than food, and the body more important than clothes?

Look at the birds of the air; they do not sow or reap or store away in barns, and yet your heavenly Father feeds them. Are you not much more valuable than they?

Who of you by worrying can add a single hour to his life?

And why do you worry about clothes? See how the lilies of the field grow. They do not labor or spin. Yet I tell you that not even Solomon in all his splendor was dressed like one of these.

If that is how God clothes the grass of the field, which is here today and tomorrow is thrown into the fire, will he not much more clothe you, O you of little faith?

So do not worry, saying, "What shall we eat?" or "What shall we drink?" or "What shall we wear?"

For the pagans run after all these things, and your heavenly Father knows that you need them.

—PHILIPPIANS 4:19; MATTHEW 6:25-32, NIV

People in America do not think it strange when a speaker from Europe asks for a collection for the work there, but I sometimes felt that there was something wrong about it.

I had been speaking on the need in the Netherlands and Germany, and after the meeting a dignified and well-dressed woman gave me money for the work in these countries.

"It was so very interesting to hear about your work," she said.

"What did you think about the other things of which I spoke? Did you find them important also?" I asked. "Of course it is a very good thing to give money for evangelistic work, but today I spoke also on conversion. God does not want only a little of our money, He wants our hearts. Because of His great love He wants to possess you completely. The Lord Jesus wants you to come to Him with all your cares, with all your sins, with all your unrest concerning the past, with all your fears about the future."

While I was speaking a haughty look came into her eyes. Very coolly, she left with no response to my comments.

When I got back to my room I looked sadly at the money she had given me. Was there perhaps something wrong in speaking of one's own work at the same time as the need for conversion? When I prayed about it the answer was very clear: *From now on you must never again ask for money.*

Great joy entered my heart and I prayed, "Heavenly Father, Thou knowest that I need more money than ever before, not only for traveling expenses and for the house in Holland, but also for the camp in Germany. But from now on the little evangelization work of the 'ten Boom Foundation' will be carried out on the same basis as the great mission work of Hudson Taylor. I know Thou wilt never forsake us."

That day I received two letters. One was from a woman in Switzerland. *Corrie, God told me that from now on you must never ask for money again,* she wrote. The other letter was from my sister in Holland. She wrote, *When I prayed for your work this morning God made it very clear to me that you should not ask anyone for financial support. He will provide everything.*

I thought of the night in the concentration camp when my sister Bep [Betsie] and I talked about our ministry plans. "Corrie, we should never waste our energy in collecting money," she said. "God is willing to supply our every need."

And now this repeated charge, in Switzerland to my friend, in Holland to my sister, and in the United States to me. God takes His prohibition on asking for money seriously, just as He means it seriously that He will care for and protect us. He is willing and able to supply our every need according to His own riches. We may trust in that promise 100 percent.

—*Amazing Love*

QUESTIONS TO CONSIDER

1. Do you trust God for the provisions, financial or otherwise, in your life? Why or why not?
2. How can you learn to trust God more?

A PRAYERFUL RESPONSE:

Lord, I am willing to trust You for the provisions in my life. Amen.

PART FOUR

THE PATH TO VICTORY

In my prison cell I gulped entire Gospels at a reading,
seeing whole the magnificent drama of salvation.
Was it possible that this war, Scheveningen prison, this very cell,
none of it was unforeseen or accidental?
Could it be part of the pattern first revealed in the Gospels?
Hadn't Jesus been defeated as utterly and unarguably
as our little underground group and our small plans had been?
But if the Gospels were truly the pattern of God's activity,
then defeat was only the beginning.
I would look around at the bare little cell and wonder
what conceivable victory could come from a place like this.

THE HIDING PLACE

CORRIE TEN BOOM'S INSIGHT

No matter the circumstances, spiritual victory belongs to God's children.

81

The Simple Truth

Thought for Today

God's way is simple, but we often complicate it.

Wisdom from Scripture

In the beginning was the Word, and the Word was with God, and the Word was God.

He was in the beginning with God.

All things came into being through him, and without him not one thing came into being. What has come into being in him was life, and the life was the light of all people.

The light shines in the darkness, and the darkness did not overcome it.

There was a man sent from God, whose name was John.

He came as a witness to testify to the light, so that all might believe through him.

He himself was not the light, but he came to testify to the light.

The true light, which enlightens everyone, was coming into the world.

He was in the world, and the world came into being through him; yet the world did not know him.

He came to what was his own, and his own people did not accept him.

But to all who received him, who believed in his name, he gave power to become children of God, who were born, not of blood or of the will of the flesh or of the will of man, but of God.

And the Word became flesh and lived among us, and we have seen his glory, the glory as of a father's only son, full of grace and truth. JOHN 1:1-14, NRSV

INSIGHTS FROM CORRIE TEN BOOM

A weekly Bible study is held in a Johannesburg post office. The walls of the beautiful lecture room resound to the music of hymns. Christians meet there together and invite all their workmates—a tremendous chance for the gospel. I find it the same in many towns in South Africa—Christians also gathering in railway buildings and insurance offices during lunch hours.

After I have spoken a girl who has a free afternoon brings me home. In the car we talk about the meeting.

"Do you know," she says, "I go every week to the lunch-hour meeting and listen with great interest, but I have never made the decision to become a Christian?"

"Have you time to stop for a moment?" I ask. "I would like to show you something in my Bible."

We park in the shade of a tree. I open the Bible and read Isaiah 53:6, "'All we like sheep have gone astray; we have turned every one to his own way.' Have you gone God's way or your own?"

"My own way," she says.

"We have all done that, but it is good that you know it," I reply. If you don't know it, I could hardly give you advice. Now read on, 'The Lord hath laid on Him the iniquity of us all.'"

I take a book in my right hand and lay it on my left.

"Look, God has taken your sins and laid them on His Son, Jesus Christ, just as I have laid this book on my left hand. This morning you heard how Jesus died on the cross to carry

84

the sins of all of us—the Lamb of God that taketh away the sins of the world."

We read together John 1:12 (KJV), "As many as received Him, to them gave He power to become the sons of God, even to them that believe on His name."

"Now, what is written there? Does He give the power to become a child of God to those who try to be good and live a better life, or to those who are members of a church? No, only to those who receive Jesus. Will you receive Him now? Jesus finished all that had to be done to make the barrier of sin disappear. Because of that God will forgive you."

She closes her eyes and prays, "Lord Jesus, will You forgive my sins? I receive you now as my Savior and Lord."

"Now we will read John 1:12 again. What are you now?"

"A child of God," she replies.

"Will you thank Him for that?"

Again she closes her eyes, "Thank You, Lord Jesus, for saving me and making me a child of God." Then she says, "What a joy now that I know it for sure. I really feel that I am now God's child."

I replied, "How often I have experienced that when we praise and give thanks, the Holy Spirit witnesses with our spirit that we are children of God. This is a joyful beginning for you. Now go forward."

On the way home she says, "How simple the way is, really."

"Yes. Complications are put there by you and me and the devil. The truth is simple, but so deep that we need the Holy Spirit to see the truth in its simplicity."

—*Not Good If Detached*

QUESTIONS TO CONSIDER
1. Why would God's way be so simple?
2. How might you simplify your approach to Him?

A PRAYERFUL RESPONSE
Lord, thank You for the simplicity of becoming Your child.
Amen.

THE POWER OF HIS NAME

THOUGHT FOR TODAY
We serve victoriously through the power of Jesus' name.

WISDOM FROM SCRIPTURE
Let the same mind be in you that was in Christ Jesus,
> who, though he was in the form of God,
>> did not regard equality with God
> as something to be exploited,
>> but emptied himself,
> taking the form of a slave,
>> being born in human likeness.
> And being found in human form,
>> he humbled himself
>> and became obedient to the point of death—
>> even death on a cross.
> Therefore God also highly exalted him
>> and gave him the name
> that is above every name,
>> so that at the name of Jesus
> every knee should bend,
>> in heaven and on earth and under the earth,
> and every tongue should confess
>> that Jesus Christ is Lord,
>> to the glory of God the Father.

Therefore, my beloved, just as you have always obeyed me, not only in my presence, but much more now in my absence, work out your own salvation with fear and trembling; for it is God who is at work in you, enabling you both to will and to work for his good pleasure.

Whoever speaks must do so as one speaking the very words of God; whoever serves must do so with the strength that God supplies, so that God may be glorified in all things through Jesus Christ. To him belong the glory and the power forever and ever. Amen.

PHILIPPIANS 2:5-13; 1 PETER 4:11, NRSV

INSIGHTS FROM CORRIE TEN BOOM

How difficult it is to speak through interpreters. It is like trying to reach for people around a corner. The listener's eyes being on the interpreter, the speaker is out of touch with his audience. It has one virtue, however: there is time for prayer while speaking.

Today I have an especially fine interpreter. He loves the Lord with all his heart and it is pure delight to work together—such a contrast to indifferent interpreters. We are guests in the same home and since we must speak again in the evening there is time to chat together.

Suddenly I ask, "Why is there so much darkness in you?"

"What do you mean?"

"There is no joy of the Lord in your eyes. In the parable of the vine and the branches, the Lord says, 'That My joy might remain in you, and that your joy might be full' (John 15:11, KJV). Where is that joy?"

"I don't know."

"I think perhaps I know. May I speak? When you were converted from Shintoism to the Lord, you turned your back on demons, but the demons have not turned their backs on you."

In surprise he answers, "That is true. But please don't tell the missionaries. They may think I've gone back to Shintoism."

"Demons are no 'ism.' They are realities even as angels, and as you and I are. What you lack is a knowledge of the riches that are yours. You need not remain in darkness one moment longer. In the name of the Lord Jesus and by the blood of the Lamb we have the victory. In His name you can drive out the demons and withstand Satan."

Together we read and obey the glorious promise and command in Mark 16:15-18, and then the Lord performs the miracle of the complete liberation of His child.

A few weeks later we meet again.

"Not only am I free," he says, "but my wife and children also."

All hail the power of Jesus' name! The wonderful name of Jesus is all powerful in heaven and on earth. That name above every name.

Many missionaries have *given* their all—money, family, and homeland—but they do not *take* all the riches offered them in God's Word. Theologically their training has been basic, but would not a study of God's Word teaching them to cast out demons and heal the sick make them more fruitful?

How many dark powers there are in the world! Yet we have nothing to fear. The fear of demons is from the demons themselves. We overcome by the blood of the Lamb, and His blood protects us. And what joy it is that we have the authority of the name of Jesus.

—*Not Good If Detached*

QUESTIONS TO CONSIDER

1. Do you believe you have the authority of Jesus' name? Why, or why not?
2. How can you incorporate this authority into your life today?

A Prayerful Response
Lord, all hail the power of Your mighty and victorious name!
Amen.

DAY 21

VICTORY OVER SIN

THOUGHT FOR TODAY
To be victorious, we confess our sin and live apart from it.

WISDOM FROM SCRIPTURE
See what love the Father has given us, that we should be called children of God; and that is what we are. The reason the world does not know us is that it did not know him.

Beloved, we are God's children now; what we will be has not yet been revealed. What we do know is this: when he is revealed, we will be like him, for we will see him as he is.

And all who have this hope in him purify themselves, just as he is pure.

Everyone who commits sin is guilty of lawlessness; sin is lawlessness.

You know that he was revealed to take away sins, and in him there is no sin.

No one who abides in him sins; no one who sins has either seen him or known him.

Little children, let no one deceive you. Everyone who does what is right is righteous, just as he is righteous.

Everyone who commits sin is a child of the devil; for the devil has been sinning from the beginning. The Son of God was revealed for this purpose, to destroy the works of the devil.

Those who have been born of God do not sin, because God's seed abides in them; they cannot sin, because they have been born of God.

—1 JOHN 3:1-9, NRSV

"Your sins have hid his face from you" (Isaiah 59:2).

We must have clear vision, but our sins often hinder us. They confuse our sight. Therefore it is important we are obedient to the command of the Lord, "Everyone who has at heart a hope like that keeps himself pure, for he knows how pure Christ is" (1 John 3:3).

He who waits for Jesus' coming gets sensitive to every shadow that comes between his Master and himself, and he does not rest until the vision is clear again. We must understand clearly that this text does not mean a striving to make ourselves better and better. We must look at Jesus, our hope. He is the Lord who sanctifies us. The Holy Spirit gives us what we need. "The Spirit . . . produces in human life fruits such as these: love, joy, peace, patience, kindness, generosity, fidelity, tolerance and self-control" (Galatians 5:22).

The devil accuses us night and day. He likes to push us into dismay, because then we cannot be strong. But the Word of God says to us, "Be strong in the Lord" (Ephesians 6:10, KJV). He can give us this command because He gives us His strength. As soon as we realize that there is a sin in our hearts, we must bring it to the Lord because that sin makes us insecure and weak.

When we confess our sins, He is faithful to forgive us our sins. We must know that the blood of Jesus cleanses us from all sins we bring to Him (see 1 John 1:7, 9). When we confess our sins to the Lord and ask for forgiveness, He will cast them into the depths of the sea. "He will turn again, he will have compassion upon us; he will subdue our iniquities; and thou wilt cast all their sins into the depths of the sea" (Micah 7:19, KJV).

He will forgive and forget, and I believe He sometimes must post a sign: "No fishing allowed!" This is necessary because sin confessed to the Lord is gone. At the cross Jesus finished everything.

Jesus is always conqueror! All we have to do is remain in good contact with Him and His life of victory will flow through us and touch the people around us. Our everyday life is our battle place. A part of God's strategy is to appoint the place where we have to fight. We cannot escape the war by looking for another front line. Our place with Him is here, under His banner of the cross! Jonah was disobedient and wanted to run away from his call, but one can never hide from God (see Jonah 1: 3).

Are you sure you are in the place where you are called? In the office, at home, at the engine, at the side of your husband or wife? Jesus gives you your place. "Abide in Me," He says, "and I in you" (John 15:4, KJV). Your place is in Him. There is no room and no time for our own plans to do private battle with the evil one, for coquetting with great or small sins of everyday life.

With Jesus hid in God! Can we find a safer hiding place? The devil will have to go first through God and Jesus before he reaches us! When soldiers are trained they receive their training in barracks together with others. The training in the victorious army of God for the last great battle does not take place under unusual circumstances, but in the midst of daily life. Here is the place of training—and everything we experience belongs to that training. So do our contacts with people.

The greatest power of God's love and joy, the fruit of the Holy Spirit, is at our disposal in daily life. What a mystery! When things are seen from the viewpoint of eternity, it makes you patient. Then you will fix your eyes upward again and again.

—*Marching Orders for the End Battle*

QUESTIONS TO CONSIDER

1. Are any sins hindering your spiritual vision? If so, will you confess them to God?
2. How can you regularly confess sin and live apart from it?

A PRAYERFUL RESPONSE

Lord, I confess my sins to You. Please forgive and cleanse me. Amen.

VICTORY THROUGH DECREASING

THOUGHT FOR TODAY

When we humble ourselves, God can use us effectively.

WISDOM FROM SCRIPTURE

They came to John and said to him, "Rabbi, the one who was with you across the Jordan, to whom you testified, here he is baptizing, and all are going to him."

John answered, "No one can receive anything except what has been given from heaven.

"You yourselves are my witnesses that I said, 'I am not the Messiah, but I have been sent ahead of him.'

"He who has the bride is the bridegroom. The friend of the bridegroom, who stands and hears him, rejoices greatly at the bridegroom's voice. For this reason my joy has been fulfilled.

"He must increase, but I must decrease."

The one who comes from above is above all; the one who is of the earth belongs to the earth and speaks about earthly things. The one who comes from heaven is above all.

He testifies to what he has seen and heard, yet no one accepts his testimony.

Whoever has accepted his testimony has certified this, that God is true.

He whom God has sent speaks the words of God, for he gives the Spirit without measure.

The Father loves the Son and has placed all things in his hands.

—JOHN 3:26-35, NRSV

"He must grow greater and I less and less" (John 3:30).

I was to work eight days in a town in Australia. The minister was difficult to work with. When we talked about the plans for the week, I was not allowed to make any decision by myself. He just dictated everything I had to do and I did try to be obedient.

When he told me he had to preach the gospel in a mental hospital, I became quite enthusiastic. I asked, "Can I go with you and work there, too?"

"Oh," he said, and looked at me unkindly. "You, a woman? Well, all right; why not? If you would like to do that, we can organize something." But after the first meeting in his church I felt we did not form a team at all. His ideas were so different from mine, it was difficult to cooperate with him.

After three days I became frightened to go with this man, with whom I was not united in spirit at all, to a place where so often there are many powers of darkness. I went to his study and said, "Pastor, I believe that I cannot go to that institution. We ought to be closely united as a team and we are not."

He became angry. "You must; you have to do what I tell you!"

I was offended and afraid. What right had this man to dictate what I had to do? But then I understood; I had to decrease still more. Someone who has lost his life for Jesus' sake cannot be offended! I prayed, "Lord, You know that I cannot do this, but I will go the lowest way. I will go the way of obedience."

It took a full hour before peace came into my heart. Then I went back and said, "Pastor, if you say I have to go, then I will do it."

"Oh, no, it is not necessary to go," he said. "I phoned the director and told him that you would not come. I simply told him, 'This Corrie ten Boom has been in a concentration camp for a time. Now she is not quite normal; we must accept that!'"

It was a relief that I did not have to go to that mental hospital, but how offended I was! I had to be on the platform with this man for another four days. People came to visit me, but they were not allowed to see me. I almost lost courage and I was afraid that it would become a lost week.

Then a young Baptist pastor who attended the meetings said to me, "I can take you to your next place tonight by car."

That was a lovely suggestion. That evening I felt I spoke with authority, although everything was difficult. I humbled myself before the people without telling them what had been my greatest problem during the whole week. When I told my host I would leave at eleven o'clock that night and the Baptist pastor would take me to the next place, he was furious. "I will take you myself tomorrow!" But I knew I had to go.

That nocturnal journey was a joy. The young minister told me what had happened in his congregation. He explained, "There were so many disagreements, so much hatred, that the Holy Spirit must have been very grieved with such a congregation; but almost all the members of my church have been in your meetings every evening and the Lord has worked! They have confessed their sins; they have put everything right. We praise and thank the Lord that He brought you here."

So it had not been wrong as I had feared. It had been difficult, but not for nothing! This experience had been an exercise to decrease so God could increase.

—*Marching Orders for the End Battle*

Questions to Consider

1. Who makes life difficult for you?
2. With this person, how can you decrease so God can increase?

A Prayerful Response

Lord, teach me to decrease so You can work through me. Amen.

VICTORY THROUGH THE BLOOD

THOUGHT FOR TODAY

There is purity and power in the blood of Jesus.

WISDOM FROM SCRIPTURE

Therefore prepare your minds for action; discipline yourselves; set all your hope on the grace that Jesus Christ will bring you when he is revealed.

Like obedient children, do not be conformed to the desires that you formerly had in ignorance.

Instead, as he who called you is holy, be holy yourselves in all your conduct; for it is written, "You shall be holy, for I am holy."

If you invoke as Father the one who judges all people impartially according to their deeds, live in reverent fear during the time of your exile.

You know that you were ransomed from the futile ways inherited from your ancestors, not with perishable things like silver or gold, but with the precious blood of Christ, like that of a lamb without defect or blemish.

He was destined before the foundation of the world, but was revealed at the end of the ages for your sake.

Through him you have come to trust in God, who raised him from the dead and gave him glory, so that your faith and hope are set on God.

Now that you have purified your souls by your obedience to the truth so that you have genuine mutual love, love one another deeply from the heart.

You have been born anew, not of perishable but of imperishable seed, through the living and enduring word of God.

—1 PETER 1:13-23, NRSV

INSIGHTS FROM CORRIE TEN BOOM

"Now they have conquered him through the blood of the Lamb, and through the Word to which they bore witness. They did not cherish life even in the face of death!" (Revelation 12:11).

Yes, the blood of Jesus Christ has great power!

There is perhaps not a word in the Bible that is so full of secret truths as the blood of Jesus. It is the secret of His incarnation, when Jesus took our flesh and blood; the secret of His obedience unto death, when He gave His blood at the cross of Calvary; the secret of His love that went beyond all understanding, when He bought us with His blood; the secret of His victory over the enemy and the secret of our eternal salvation.

Why does the devil hate this word? Because it reminds him of his defeat on Calvary by the death of Jesus who gave His blood for us, but also reminds him of Jesus' life, the Resurrected One, to whom we may come with our sins. That is why the devil is afraid of it. The blood of Jesus Christ has great power.

Once I visited a big prison in Manila. It was a hotbed of sin. There were seven thousand prisoners. I had an opportunity to speak there during three afternoons and when I entered I noticed that above the door was written: *Security Limit.* I asked what that meant and was told when anyone entered this prison he had to go at his own risk because there were only a few guards.

I looked into my heart to see if I was afraid—and yes, I must admit there was much fear! But what could I do? I knew I was in the way of the Lord, so I must obey!

When I came to the inner court, a great surprise was waiting for me. There was a band of about ninety musicians. When they saw me they started to play, "There is power, wonder-working power in the precious blood of the Lamb!" All my fear disappeared.

There is no reason to be afraid when a child of God is under the protection of the blood of the Lamb, the blood of Jesus. God gave us a great blessing. Three times I reached seven thousand men with the help of a loudspeaker. I reached them with the rich gospel, the glad tidings for sinners.

—*Marching Orders for the End Battle*

QUESTIONS TO CONSIDER
1. How can you grow confident in the power of Jesus' blood?
2. What aspects of your life need this power today?

A PRAYERFUL RESPONSE
Lord, I believe there is power in Your blood. Protect me with it. Amen.

DAY 24

VICTORY THROUGH THE SPIRIT

THOUGHT FOR TODAY

When we surrender to God, we increase the Spirit's fullness within.

WISDOM FROM SCRIPTURE

[Jesus said,] "For everyone who asks receives, and everyone who searches finds, and for everyone who knocks, the door will be opened.

"Is there anyone among you who, if your child asks for a fish, will give a snake instead of a fish? Or if the child asks for an egg, will give a scorpion?

"If you then, who are evil, know how to give good gifts to your children, how much more will the heavenly Father give the Holy Spirit to those who ask him!"

After his suffering he presented himself alive to them by many convincing proofs, appearing to them during forty days and speaking about the kingdom of God.

While staying with them, he ordered them not to leave Jerusalem, but to wait there for the promise of the Father. "This," he said, "is what you have heard from me; for John baptized with water, but you will be baptized with the Holy Spirit not many days from now."

So when they had come together, they asked him, "Lord, is this the time when you will restore the kingdom to Israel?"

He replied, "It is not for you to know the times or periods that the Father has set by his own authority. But you will receive power when the Holy Spirit has come upon you; and you will be my witnesses in Jerusalem, in all Judea and Samaria, and to the ends of the earth."

LUKE 11:10-13; ACTS 1:3-8, NRSV

"You are to be given power when the Holy Spirit has come to you. You will be witnesses to me, not only in Jerusalem, not only throughout Judea, not only in Samaria, but to the very ends of the earth!" (Acts 1:8). This power of the Holy Spirit is of tremendous value to us. The Bible says, "Be filled with the Spirit!" (Ephesians 5:18, NRSV).

In Holland a woman started a prayer meeting in her room. Her brother had not much faith about it and said, "You will never succeed!"

But the next day she told him, "My room was full up!"

"All right," he said. "But just wait and see what happens next week!"

But the next time she said, "My room was even fuller."

And the third time: "Now it was fuller still!"

Her brother said, "That is impossible. When your room is full, it cannot be fuller."

"Oh, yes," she said. "Every week we took some more furniture out of the room."

When we are filled with the Holy Spirit, then another step may be necessary. It is possible that some "furniture" must be removed from the heart: television, some books, friendships, personal hobbies—everything that can hinder us from following Jesus Christ. We can clear out still more for Jesus, so we can make room for the Holy Spirit.

My glove cannot do anything by itself, but when my hand is in the glove, it can do a great deal. It can cook, write, and do many things! I know that it is not the glove, but the hand in the glove. When I put only one finger in the glove, it cannot do anything!

So it is with us. We are gloves; the Holy Spirit is the hand which can do everything, but we must give Him room right into the outer corners of our lives. Then we can expect that He will do a lot in and through us. In John 14:17 it is written, "He is with you and will be in your hearts!"

"So, if you, with all your evil, know how to give good things to your children, how much more likely is it that your heavenly Father will give the Holy Spirit to those who ask him!" (Luke 11:13).

John the Baptist has said, "The one who comes after me… will baptize you with the Holy Spirit and with fire" (Matthew 3:11). Jesus is the baptizer and the fullness of the Holy Spirit is the birthright of every child of God.

—Marching Orders for the End Times

QUESTIONS TO CONSIDER
1. What "furniture" do you need to remove from your soul?
2. Are you filled with the Holy Spirit? How do you know?

A PRAYERFUL RESPONSE
Lord, I empty myself so Your Spirit can dwell fully within me. Amen.

Victory Through Surrender

Thought for Today

If we surrender to Him, God uses our mistakes for His honor.

Wisdom from Scripture

But if we hope for what we do not see, we wait for it with patience.

Likewise the Spirit helps us in our weakness; for we do not know how to pray as we ought, but that very Spirit intercedes with sighs too deep for words.

And God, who searches the heart, knows what is the mind of the Spirit, because the Spirit intercedes for the saints according to the will of God.

We know that all things work together for good for those who love God, who are called according to his purpose.

For those whom he foreknew he also predestined to be conformed to the image of his Son, in order that he might be the firstborn within a large family.

And those whom he predestined he also called; and those whom he called he also justified; and those whom he justified he also glorified.

What then are we to say about these things? If God is for us, who is against us?

He who did not withhold his own Son, but gave him up for all of us, will he not with him also give us everything else?

Who will bring any charge against God's elect? It is God who justifies.

Who is to condemn? It is Christ Jesus, who died, yes, who was raised, who is at the right hand of God, who indeed intercedes for us.

Who will separate us from the love of Christ? Will hardship, or distress, or persecution, or famine, or nakedness, or peril, or sword?

No, in all these things we are more than conquerors through him who loved us.

—ROMANS 8:25-35, 37, NRSV

INSIGHTS FROM CORRIE TEN BOOM

"Who shall also confirm you unto the end, that ye may be blameless in the day of our Lord Jesus Christ" (1 Corinthians 1:8, KJV).

Are you prepared for the coming of Jesus? Am I prepared for the coming of Jesus? It is wonderful that it is written so clearly in the Bible: it is only by full surrender that we are made ready for His coming again. If it depended on us, then one day we would be successful, but the next day just the opposite.

William Nagenda, an evangelist from Uganda, has a good example of what surrender means. One day he arrived home after a long trip. There his three-year-old son stood at the station waiting for him.

"Daddy, I will carry your suitcase," he said.

William did not want to disappoint him and said, "All right, put your hand on my hand." So the little boy kept his weak little hand on the hand of his father. They came home and the little boy said, "Mummy, I carried Daddy's suitcase."

So it is with us. Our hands are not strong enough, but when we lay our weak hand on the strong hand of Jesus, He prepares us for His coming again. We must not forget "that the One who has begun his good work in you will go on developing it until the day of Jesus Christ" (Philippians 1:6).

We shall not be so ignorant as the little boy and say, "I carried the suitcase!" We shall honor the Lord for all this. We shall see Jesus face to face, and it is important whether we shall see Him as our judge or as our redeemer. Have you put your weak hand on the strong hand of your Savior? Do you believe that Jesus can help you? Paul says, "For I know the one in whom I have placed my confidence, and I am perfectly certain that the work he has committed to me is safe in his hands until that day" (2 Timothy 1:12).

There is still a tremendous struggle and fight, but the moment comes when our sanctification is complete. In 1 Thessalonians 3:12-13, it says, "May the Lord give you the same increasing and overflowing love for each other and towards all men as we have towards you. May he establish you, holy and blameless in heart and soul, before God, the Father of us all."

Yes, the best is yet to be! One day there will be an end to the battle. Then there will be the victory, victory through Jesus Christ! "May the God of peace make you holy through and through. May you be kept in soul and mind and body in spotless integrity until the coming of our Lord Jesus Christ" (1 Thessalonians 5:23).

Full surrender also includes our mistakes and errors. Once somebody visited a weavers' school. He asked one of the pupils, "What do you do when you have made a mistake? Can you cut it out, or must you start from the very beginning?"

The pupil said, "No, our teacher is such a great artist that when we make a mistake, he uses that to increase the beauty of the pattern." That is what Jesus does with us! Our feeling of inferiority is really pride, because we will not accept that our ability is limited. We want to be better than we really are.

But it is so wonderful that when we acknowledge our mistakes, the Lord sometimes uses them to His honor.

When there is total surrender, then we walk relaxed in the hand of the Savior.

—Marching Orders for the End Battle

QUESTIONS TO CONSIDER
1. Today, how will you place your hand in God's hand?
2. What mistakes will you surrender to God?

A PRAYERFUL RESPONSE
Lord, I surrender myself and my mistakes to You. Amen.

Victory Through Jesus' Name

Thought for Today

In Jesus' name, we can perform miracles.

Wisdom from Scripture

He said to them, "The harvest is plentiful, but the laborers are few; therefore ask the Lord of the harvest to send out laborers into his harvest.

"Go on your way. See, I am sending you out like lambs into the midst of wolves.

"Carry no purse, no bag, no sandals; and greet no one on the road.

"Whatever house you enter, first say, 'Peace to this house!'

"And if anyone is there who shares in peace, your peace will rest on that person; but if not, it will return to you.

"Remain in the same house, eating and drinking whatever they provide, for the laborer deserves to be paid. Do not move about from house to house.

"Whenever you enter a town and its people welcome you, eat what is set before you; cure the sick who are there, and say to them. 'The kingdom of God has come near to you.'

"But whenever you enter a town and they do not welcome you, go out into its streets and say, 'Even the dust of your town that clings to our feet, we wipe off in protest against you. Yet know this: the kingdom of God has come near.'

"Whoever listens to you listens to me, and whoever rejects you rejects me, and whoever rejects me rejects the one who sent me."

The seventy returned with joy, saying, "Lord, in your name even the demons submit to us!"

He said to them, "I watched Satan fall from heaven like a flash of lightening.

"See, I have given you authority to tread on snakes and scorpions, and over all the power of the enemy; and nothing will hurt you.

"Nevertheless, do not rejoice at this, that the spirits submit to you, but rejoice that your names are written in heaven." —LUKE 10:2-11, 16-20, NRSV

INSIGHTS FROM CORRIE TEN BOOM

The name of Jesus is wonderful!

Once I heard a story of a sick lady in Germany. A friend asked her, "Do you know it is written in the Bible that Jesus said, 'They will lay their hands upon the sick and they will recover'?" Then he read Mark 16 and asked, "Do you believe the Bible?"

"Yes," she said, "I believe the whole Bible." Then he laid his hands on her and she was healed. She was so happy that she went to her pastor and said, "Did you know that text is in the Bible?"

The pastor's answer was, "I am sorry, but I must tell you that that part of Mark 16 was added to the Bible long, long afterward." One moment she was very disappointed, but suddenly her eyes started to beam with joy and she said, "What a wonderful book is the Bible, that even an added promise has so much power that I was healed!"

Yes, when we believe the rich treasures of the Bible, we experience that God, who gave us all these promises, really keeps them. The name of Jesus is a wonderful name. The Bible not only teaches us that we can pray in this name, but that we should pray in Jesus' name.

Once I heard a very good example of this from my friend William Nagenda, an African brother. He told me about a letter that his wife wrote him when he was abroad. Their little boy, aged three, asked, "Mummy, what are you doing?"

"I am writing a letter to Daddy."

"I will write a letter to Daddy, too."

She gave him a piece of paper and a pencil and then he made all kinds of scrawls. "This is my letter to Daddy," the boy said. The mother wrote under all these scrawls, "This is Christopher's letter to Daddy."

When we pray, it doesn't matter whether it is a beautiful prayer, or a prayer from our prayer book, or perhaps just a cry of distress directly to the Lord. It is never good enough for the holy God. But when we say, "In the name of Jesus," then it is just as if Jesus says, "Father, this prayer is from Your child" and then the heavenly Father is delighted with our prayer! That prayer is sanctified by the name of Jesus.

Use this name! Not the name of Christ; that is His title. The name that is above every name in heaven or on earth is the name of Jesus, our Savior! He is our strength. That name brings all of heaven and earth together. One cannot overestimate the value of that name in the great final battle.

—*Marching Orders for the End Battle*

QUESTIONS TO CONSIDER

1. Why would Jesus require that we call on His name for power?
2. How can you exercise the power of Jesus' name today?

A PRAYERFUL RESPONSE

Lord, teach me the power and victory of Your name. Amen.

PART FIVE

THE PRIVILEGE OF SERVICE

It took a lot of love.

The most pressing need in postwar Germany was homes;
nine million people were said to be without them.

They were living in rubble heaps, half-standing buildings,
and abandoned army trucks.

A church group invited me to speak to a hundred families
living in an abandoned factory building.

Sheets and blankets hung between the various living quarters
to make a pretense of privacy.

How could I speak to these people of the reality of God
and then go back to my quiet room in the church hostel
outside the city?

No, before I could bring a message to them,
I would live among them.

THE HIDING PLACE

CORRIE TEN BOOM'S INSIGHT

We can serve one another with the love Christ shed in our hearts.

NOT WITHOUT ME

THOUGHT FOR TODAY

God's work is to be accomplished with His direction.

WISDOM FROM SCRIPTURE

Do not worry about anything, but in everything by prayer and supplication with thanksgiving let your requests be made known to God.

And the peace of God, which surpasses all understanding, will guard your hearts and your minds in Christ Jesus.

Finally, beloved, whatever is true, whatever is honorable, whatever is just, whatever is pure, whatever is pleasing, whatever is commendable, if there is any excellence and if there is anything worthy of praise, think about these things.

Keep on doing the things that you have learned and received and heard and seen in me, and the God of peace will be with you.

For I have learned to be content with whatever I have.

I know what it is to have little, and I know what it is to have plenty. In any and all circumstances I have learned the secret of being well-fed and of going hungry, of having plenty and of being in need.

I can do all things through him who strengthens me.

—PHILIPPIANS 4:6-9, 11-13, NRSV

INSIGHTS FROM CORRIE TEN BOOM

A friend asked me if I could go to Bermuda for a week, so I asked the Lord for guidance. When it became clear He wanted me to go, I wrote immediately to Bermuda, saying I would come. Within two or three days checks arrived from different people and there was enough money for a return ticket.

It was the beginning of a week of blessing such as I had never experienced before. My schedule was more than filled. There were at least twenty speaking engagements. Whenever I spoke, I felt myself upheld by the prayers of my friends in the United States, who were in sympathy with me and who expected much of this work.

The first morning a young man came to interview me for the press. We prayed together and he became an important and loyal helper in the work. He was present at all twenty meetings and each day there was an excellent and accurate report of my messages. My talks became known to many who had not been to the meetings and that created possibilities for other, less formal contacts.

What was the happiest experience of this blessed week? The privilege of dispensing the great riches of God's Word to people who did not tire of listening to it. I prayed, "Oh, Lord, do let me have more experiences such as this one."

Then came Cleveland. I was staying with friends, but there was not much opportunity to speak in their church: one evening meeting, poorly attended, and I spoke for fifteen minutes to the children in the Sunday school. I was discontented. Compared with this, Bermuda knew how to appreciate Corrie ten Boom.

Chicago was next on my schedule, but no word had come to confirm my appointments there. I decided, without waiting for guidance, that I could go a day later. There were some unexpected opportunities to speak in Cleveland, so I sent a telegram to Chicago to inform them I would arrive two days later.

A friend was waiting at the station in Chicago when I arrived. "Why didn't you come at the appointed time?" was his first question. "You have missed two important engagements."

Startled, and also a bit chagrined, I answered, "Why didn't you write and confirm our arrangements?"

"We couldn't. You failed to send us your Cleveland address."

Everything in Chicago went further and further awry. I missed connections and seemed to do the wrong thing at every turn. I was glad when the time came for me to leave for Michigan. The first evening with my friends there we talked and talked.

"How was Bermuda?"

"Oh, wonderful! What a place! Such lovely people!"

"And how was Cleveland?"

"Oh, nothing out of the ordinary." And I began to speak again about Bermuda.

"And Chicago?"

"An awful place to be in the summer. Stiflingly hot, both night and day."

That evening I had a long talk with the Lord. "Lord, go back with me to Chicago and Cleveland. What was wrong there?" The answer was very clear: *Cleveland and Chicago, that was Corrie ten Boom without Me. Bermuda, that was Corrie with Me.*

Now I could see it. "Without Me ye can do nothing," said the Lord (John 15:5, KJV). "I can do all things through [Christ] who strengthens me," said Paul (Philippians 4:13, NRSV). The branch of the vine, without Him, bears no fruit at all, but with Him, much fruit.

—*Amazing Love*

QUESTIONS TO CONSIDER
1. Are you serving others *for* God or *with* Him?
2. How can you begin serving others, with God's guidance?

A PRAYERFUL RESPONSE
Lord, please strengthen and guide me to serve others. Amen.

WALKING IN THE LIGHT

THOUGHT FOR TODAY
Walking in God's light means giving Him our all.

WISDOM FROM SCRIPTURE
We declare to you what was from the beginning, what we have heard, what we have seen with our eyes, what we have looked at and touched with our hands, concerning the word of life—this life was revealed, and we have seen it and testify to it, and declare to you the eternal life that was with the Father and was revealed to us—we declare to you what we have seen and heard so that you also may have fellowship with us; and truly our fellowship is with the Father and with his Son Jesus Christ.

We are writing these things so that our joy may be complete.

This is the message we have heard from him and proclaim to you, that God is light and in him there is no darkness at all.

If we say that we have fellowship with him while we are walking in darkness, we lie and do not do what is true; but if we walk in the light as he himself is in the light, we have fellowship with one another, and the blood of Jesus his Son cleanses us from all sin.

—1 JOHN 1:1-7, NRSV

INSIGHTS FROM CORRIE TEN BOOM
I was speaking at an American university on the subject of evangelism.

"If I straighten the pictures on the walls of your house, I

am committing no sin, am I? But suppose your house were afire and I still calmly straightened pictures, what would you say? Would you think me merely stupid or wicked? Why, you'd say I was not only stupid but wicked as well.

"The world today is on fire. What are you doing to extinguish the fire? Are you sitting in your study formulating theological concepts? Are you in training for a tennis tournament? These things are good in themselves, but what are you doing to put out the fire? A Communist has written, 'The only people who can help the world in its present condition are the Christians, but they do not realize it.'

"Has Jesus not said, 'You are the salt of the earth...the light of the world' (Matthew 5:13-14)? The children of light!"

The next morning I was walking in the garden of the beautiful campus with a co-ed. "Tell me," I said, "What are you doing to bring the gospel to students?"

Her lovely face colored as she said, "I feel guilty this morning. I see myself as the fireman who goes around straightening pictures while the house burns. I am a very self-conscious person. I have given my heart to Jesus and I know I am a child of God. But there is still a part of my shy self living within an enclosure deep inside me and I become furious with anyone who approaches that enclosure. I have always felt that I had a right to live my own life. Recently I gave my testimony at our club meeting and they told me that my language and style and voice were quite good. So I know I could speak in public. But if I do, people will see behind the enclosure, and that I will not have."

"Jeannie, it is only when we are crucified with Christ that we can enter into the joy of His resurrection. That sounds bad, but it is a loss that turns out to be a great gain. You will find His yoke is easy and His burden light. The time is short. To be lost for eternity is a dreadful thing, and to be used in saving others is a wonderful experience."

I once heard a sermon by Oswald Smith at a conference in Switzerland. He held four books in his hands and asked, "Is everything on the altar? Have you lost your life for Christ's sake, your money, your time, your family, your home?"

He placed the four books on the table, "This is my money; this, my time; this, my family; this, my home. Yes, my money, all of it, except a small savings account which I have laid aside for my vacation.

"So, not all of my money." And he took one book from the table.

"My home, yes, except that I cannot take the children of my sister who is ill. They are so unruly I can't have them as guests in my home.

"So, not my home." And he removed the second book from the table.

"My time? Yes, it all belongs to the Lord. But my two weeks of vacation? I have a right to that and have already reserved a room at the hotel.

"So, not my time." A third book disappeared.

"My family, yes, but I have not allowed my daughter to become what she so eagerly wishes to be: a missionary. We have a large family, and she must help her mother.

"So, not my family." He picked up the fourth book. The altar was empty.

I left the conference room and searched my heart. Was everything in my life on the altar? I understood what Oswald Smith meant. It was not a question of God's permitting His children to have their vacations. Rather, it was "seek ye first the kingdom of God, and His righteousness; and all these things shall be added unto you" (Matthew 6:33, KJV). "Everything, Lord, except this one thing" will not do.

—Amazing Love

QUESTIONS TO CONSIDER
1. Are you walking in God's light or in the darkness? Explain.
2. In order to walk in the light, what do you still need to give to God?

A PRAYERFUL RESPONSE
Lord, I will surrender all so I can walk in Your light. Amen.

SMALL MOMENTS, GREAT WORKS

THOUGHT FOR TODAY

God accomplishes great works in small moments.

WISDOM FROM SCRIPTURE

Jesus said to him, "I am the way, and the truth, and the life. No one comes to the Father except through me.

"If you know me, you will know my Father also. From now on you do know him and have seen him."

Philip said to him, "Lord, show us the Father, and we will be satisfied."

Jesus said to him, "Have I been with you all this time, Philip, and you still do not know me? Whoever has seen me has seen the Father. How can you say, 'Show us the Father'?

"Do you not believe that I am in the Father and the Father is in me? The words that I say to you I do not speak on my own; but the Father who dwells in me does his works.

"Believe me that I am in the Father and the Father is in me; but if you do not, then believe me because of the works themselves.

"Very truly, I tell you, the one who believes in me will also do the works that I do and, in fact, will do greater works than these, because I am going to the Father.

"I will do whatever you ask in my name, so that the Father may be glorified in the Son.

"If in my name you ask me for anything, I will do it."

—JOHN 14:6-14, NRSV

In a Bermuda prison I see a crouching figure, a red patch on the back of his prison uniform.

"Has he tried to escape?" I ask the attendant.

"Yes, but how did you know? This is a tragic case. The man, a murderer, was sentenced to be flogged. He feared the beating so much, he tried to run away. Now he has had to bear double punishment."

I pray, "Lord, help me find the way to reach this man's heart."

My own prison experiences come to mind. When our fellow prisoners were tortured we urged them to tell us all that had happened. It was hard listening, but it helped them to throw off their terrible experience. If it is possible to get this man to talk, perhaps I can find the way to his heart.

"Hello! Did you have a beating?" I ask.

"Yes."

"Was it bad?"

"Yes."

"Come, tell me. Did they take you to the hospital afterward?"

"No, it wasn't that bad." He comes to the barred door and looks at me with wondering eyes. What kind of woman asks such questions?

And my heart says, *Thank You, God. He is already at the door!*

"Didn't they do anything for you?"

"Yes, they rubbed me with salve."

Then I inquire, "Is there hate in your heart?"

"Hate! I am full of hate."

"This is something I can understand."

"You?"

"Certainly. I know how you feel." Then I tell him of the

beatings I had in Ravensbruck and, even worse, the beatings given to my weak sister Betsie because she no longer had the strength to shovel dirt. Then hatred tried to enter into my heart, but a miracle happened, for Jesus filled my heart with God's love, and there was no room for hatred.

Then I say, "If you will accept Him as your Savior, He will do the same for you."

It is a struggle between life and death, but life wins. He utters "yes" to Jesus, and the angels in heaven rejoice. We pray together, and he offers a stammering prayer. Then we shake hands through the bars.

Sometimes I am asked, "Can people really be saved so quickly?"

I always answer, "How long did it take Levi, the tax collector? Jesus said, 'Follow Me,' and he promptly closed his office and followed the Lord."

"Yes, but that was Jesus."

"Who do you suppose it was in the Bermuda prison? Do you think it was Corrie ten Boom who converted that man? No, it was Jesus who has said, 'Verily, verily, I say unto you, He that believeth on Me, the works that I do shall he do also; and greater works than these shall he do; because I go unto My Father'" (John 14:12, KJV).

—Not Good If Detached

QUESTIONS TO CONSIDER

1. How can you become aware of small moments to serve others?
2. How can you measure the effectiveness of these small moments?

A Prayerful Response

Lord, keep me attuned to the small moments available for service. Amen.

TELL ME OF JESUS

THOUGHT FOR TODAY

No matter their place in society, all people need Jesus.

WISDOM FROM SCRIPTURE

Of course, there is great gain in godliness combined with contentment; for we brought nothing into the world, so that we can take nothing out of it; but if we have food and clothing, we will be content with these.

But those who want to be rich fall into temptation and are trapped by many senseless and harmful desires that plunge people into ruin and destruction.

For the love of money is a root of all kinds of evil, and in their eagerness to be rich some have wandered away from the faith and pierced themselves with many pains.

But as for you, man of God, shun all this; pursue righteousness, godliness, faith, love, endurance, gentleness.

Fight the good fight of the faith; take hold of the eternal life, to which you were called and for which you made the good confession in the presence of many witnesses.

As for those who in the present age are rich, command them not to be haughty, or to set their hopes on the uncertainty of riches, but rather on God who richly provides us with everything for our enjoyment.

They are to do good, to be rich in good works, generous, and ready to share, thus storing up for themselves the treasure of a good foundation for the future, so that they may take hold of the life that really is life.

—1 TIMOTHY 6:6-12, 17-19, NRSV

On the platform the choir, in brownish-red gowns, stands behind me; a lady in a white gown is conducting. I study her while she conducts the choir. She wears a lot of jewelry and gracefully moves her beautiful arms, which are decorated with diamond bracelets. She wears brilliant rings on her fingers; her nails are red. Her shoes are transparent. She smiles coquettishly when the tenors make a mistake, encouragingly when a passage is difficult, and coquettishly again when she has nothing else to do.

It is strange to see such a worldly woman taking part in a sacred service. Looking at her, she appears to me to be representative of the movie world, where coquettish women play a big part. Suddenly she sings together with the choir. She has a beautiful voice. Although she stands with her back to the congregation, her solo can be heard above the voices of the choir.

For a time I am so absorbed in her appearance that I do not hear what they are singing. Now I listen to the words. She sings, "Tell me of Jesus."

My mind wanders. I am no longer in the church. Those words go round and round in my mind. Hollywood demands, "Tell me of Jesus." The sentenced-to-death, desperate, painted society asks, "Tell me of Jesus."

When moments later I stand before the congregation to bring them my message, in my heart there is a longing—a prayer. *Let me, this woman, and the movie world in Hollywood, tell of Jesus—of Him who came because the Father loved this poor, bad, desperate world.*

Because of my background of imprisonment and world traveling, I sometimes arrive at places where doors do not open easily. I stand before a hearth. In front of me sit fifty movie stars. The Hollywood Christian Group is having its gospel meeting. About twenty of their members are present; the rest are friends and acquaintances who do not yet know the Lord. We are in the house of a rich movie star. One of those present has a strong lamp which she focuses on me and studies the effect.

I speak about the great love of God in Jesus Christ who can lift us out of the old vicious circle of sin and death. The Holy Spirit convinces us of sin, righteousness, and judgment. The greatest sin is not believing in Jesus.

After the meeting little groups of people form. I see that the Christians are active and busy with open Bibles, showing their colleagues the way of salvation.

I go with a young woman for a little walk on the terrace. She has many questions to ask. Passing a window I see two young men on their knees. One is a member of the Christian Group, the other a movie star who is making the decision that makes angels rejoice.

Everyone needs Jesus.

—Not Good If Detached

Questions to Consider
1. Think of your friends and acquaintances. Who doesn't seem to need Jesus?
2. How can you tell this person about the Lord?

A Prayerful Response
Lord, motivate me to tell self-sufficient people about You. Amen.

DAY 31

PLENTY FOR EVERYONE

THOUGHT FOR TODAY

The blessings of God are plenty for everyone.

WISDOM FROM SCRIPTURE

When they [the disciples] had gone ashore, they saw a charcoal fire there, with fish on it, and bread.

Jesus said to them, "Bring some of the fish that you have just caught."

So Simon Peter went aboard and hauled the net ashore, full of large fish, a hundred fifty-three of them; and though there were so many, the net was not torn.

Jesus said to them, "Come and have breakfast." Now none of the disciples dared to ask him, "Who are you?" because they knew it was the Lord.

Jesus came and took the bread and gave it to them, and did the same with the fish.

This was now the third time that Jesus appeared to the disciples after he was raised from the dead.

When they had finished breakfast, Jesus said to Simon Peter, "Simon son of John, do you love me more than these?" He said to him, "Yes, Lord; you know that I love you." Jesus said to him, "Feed my lambs."

A second time he said to him, "Simon son of John, do you love me?" He said to him, "Yes, Lord; you know that I love you." Jesus said to him, "Tend my sheep."

He said to him the third time, "Simon son of John, do you love me?" Peter felt hurt because he said to him the third time, "Do you love me?" And he said to him, "Lord, you know everything; you know that I love you." Jesus said to him, "Feed my sheep."

—John 21:9-17, NRSV

Insights from Corrie ten Boom

When the disciples were passing out food to the five thousand they must have rejoiced in their hearts, seeing the miracle. Plenty for everyone. When a Christian receives Bible messages, straight from the hands of Jesus, he too experiences plenty for everyone.

My personal contact with people is often too brief. Although I like to do more thorough work and speak at least six times to the same audience, I am often permitted to speak only once to a group of people. Then I grumble and feel unhappy. Nevertheless I see how the Lord blesses these once-only meetings. Then I must thank Him and repent of my grumbling. I have no other choice; I must obey.

I am so rich. I have a book, the Bible: what a book! It is full of rich promises, blessings, realities—full of our Savior, Jesus Christ. I have the privilege to share this good news of plenty almost every day with people in different parts of the world. Not many are called to the same kind of traveling service. Only after my fifty-fourth year did God ordain me. Before that time I lived for more than fifty years in the same house in Holland.

But it is not such a great difference to speak to people in your homeland as anywhere else in the world. Every Christian is called to be on duty twenty-four hours every day in the King's business. Your office, your school, your kitchen, your drawing-room, your factory, all are a mission field. Jesus still says, "Give the hungry to eat."

Dr. Billy Graham has said, "We are debtors. We owe the world the gospel." Yes, we can do nothing more important than share the Good News of Jesus. It is our only response to the Lord in thankfulness for our plentiful salvation.

I once read a legend about Christ's return to heaven, when He had finished His work in this world. As He arrived at the shore of heaven the angels ran to meet Him, eagerly questioning Him about His work on earth among men.

"Did you complete your work of redemption?"

"Yes, it is finished."

"Who will make it known?"

"I have told Peter, John, Philip, and all who are My disciples."

"And what if they fail?"

"I have no other plan, and they will not fail."

How is it that Jesus can trust to our care the important task of taking the gospel to the lost all over the world? The grand answer is that He has given us all that is necessary for the task. The Holy Spirit is there to give us power. In Acts 1:8 (Amplified) we read, "But you shall receive power—ability, efficiency and might—when the Holy Spirit has come upon you." Following this promise is the order to march: "And you shall be My witnesses in Jerusalem and all Judea and Samaria and to the ends—the very bounds—of the earth."

He has also given us the boundless resources of the Bible, a book of Good News, and plenty of it! It gives the answers to all the problems of mankind. If we stand before the "plenty" of God's great riches our amazement is more at the grace of God which enables us to be channels of all His love and goodness.

And so I set out. He said, "Go ye" (Matthew 28:19, KJV). He has given me His plenty and provided His mighty power to feed the world's multitudes. Come with me and see some of the great things the Lord has done.

—Plenty for Everyone

QUESTIONS TO CONSIDER

1. How have you answered the Lord's command, "Feed My sheep"?
2. How have you experienced that there is "plenty for everyone"?

A PRAYERFUL RESPONSE

Lord, I will feed Your sheep and believe there is plenty for everyone. Amen.

DAY 32

TRAMP FOR THE LORD

THOUGHT FOR TODAY
God wants our service for a lifetime.

WISDOM FROM SCRIPTURE
Who will separate us from the love of Christ? Will hardship, or distress, or persecution, or famine, or nakedness, or peril, or sword?

As it is written,

"For your sake we are being killed all day long;

we are accounted as sheep to be slaughtered."

No, in all these things we are more than conquerors through him who loved us.

For I am convinced that neither death, nor life, nor angels, nor rulers, nor things present, nor things to come, nor powers, nor height, nor depth, nor anything else in all creation, will be able to separate us from the love of God in Christ Jesus our Lord.

—ROMANS 8:35-39, NRSV

INSIGHTS FROM CORRIE TEN BOOM
In my journeys I often cross borders between countries and knowing that smuggling is sin, I do not do it. So an irritation came through an encounter with a customs official when he asked me if I had anything to declare.

I replied, "Yes, nylon stockings," and put them on top of my luggage to show him.

"There are four pairs here," he said. "You told me one pair!"

"No, I did not."

He took my suitcases and gave them such a thorough inspection it took at least an hour. He tried all the little boxes for false bottoms. I felt offended and unhappy. He found nothing, so I paid the duty on the four pairs of stockings, but the depression and unhappiness remained. Then I discovered I missed my plane connection and was forced to sleep on a couch in the women's room at the airport. Eventually the plane I did catch flew into a storm, making me feel airsick. The night following my arrival there was an earthquake.

The people who would have arranged my meetings greeted my arrival with, "We thought you needed a holiday and a rest so we have not organized anything." Sometimes I am given this sort of encouragement, but it is often an excuse for their inactivity, which I do not appreciate. The room my hosts gave me was small, without a table for writing.

Self-pity entered my heart. This time it began, *Why must you always live out of your suitcases? Stay at home and then you won't have trouble with customs officials, passports, luggage, plane connections, and other things. Every night you will be able to sleep in the same comfortable bed and there are no earthquakes in Holland. After all, you are no longer young: you've lived like a tramp for fifteen years. Nobody is indispensable; let someone else do the work. There's plenty for you to do in Holland.*

Having listened to this self-pity, I wrote to Bloemendaal, where my friend was manager of an international guest house and where I had a room with all my own furniture. I wrote: *I believe the time has now come for me to work in Holland. I am tired of all this traveling and I cannot stand having wheels beneath me any longer. Will you arrange to have a desk—a big one—put in front of the window in my room, and an easy chair—a very easy one—on the right....* Everyone would know that I needed to go home.

135

Everything would have gone all right—or perhaps it would be truthful to say all wrong—had I not read from one of Amy Carmichael's books that evening. Do you know her story, or rather dream, which the Lord gave her in India? Toward the end, this happened:

Then I saw, like a little picture of peace, a group of people under some trees, with their backs turned toward the gulf. They were making daisy chains. Sometimes when a piercing shriek cut the quiet air and reached them it disturbed them, and they thought it rather a vulgar noise. And if one of their number started up and wanted to go and do something to help, then all the others would pull that one down.

"Why should you get so excited about it? You must wait for a definite call to go! You have not finished your daisy chains yet. It would be really selfish," they said, "to leave us to finish the work alone."

Then thundered a voice, the Voice of the Lord. And He said, "What hast thou done? The voice of my brothers' blood crieth unto Me from the ground."

Tom-toms beat heavily, darkness shuddered and shivered about me; I heard the yells of devil-dancers and the weird wild shriek of the devil-possessed just outside the gate. "What does it matter, after all? It has gone on for years; it will go on for years. Why make such a fuss about it?"

God forgive us! God arouse! Shame us out of our callousness! Shame us out of our sin!

After I finished reading I sent another letter to Holland: *Forget what I wrote in my last letter; I hope to die in the harness.*
—*Plenty for Everyone*

QUESTIONS TO CONSIDER
1. How are you sometimes tempted to give up serving God?
2. How can you overcome this temptation?

A PRAYERFUL RESPONSE
Lord, I want to serve You all the days of my life. Amen.

SERVING AS UNTO HIM

THOUGHT FOR TODAY
When we serve others, we serve God.

WISDOM FROM SCRIPTURE

[Jesus said,] "When the Son of Man comes in his glory, and all the angels with him, then he will sit on the throne of his glory.

"All the nations will be gathered before him, and he will separate people one from another as a shepherd separates the sheep from the goats, and he will put the sheep at his right hand and the goats at the left.

"Then the king will say to those at his right hand, 'Come, you that are blessed by my Father, inherit the kingdom prepared for you from the foundation of the world; for I was hungry and you gave me food, I was thirsty and you gave me something to drink, I was a stranger and you welcomed me, I was naked and you gave me clothing, I was sick and you took care of me, I was in prison and you visited me.'

"Then the righteous will answer him, 'Lord, when was it that we saw you hungry and gave you food, or thirsty and gave you something to drink?

"'And when was it that we saw you a stranger and welcomed you, or naked and gave you clothing?

"'And when was it that we saw you sick or in prison and visited you?'

"And the king will answer them, 'Truly I tell you, just as you did it to one of the least of these who are members of my family, you did it to me.'" MATTHEW 25:31-40, NRSV

My father often said, "My name is on the shop, but it would be proper to have God's name on the window. I am a watchmaker by the grace of God. It is God's watchmaker's shop." When we start to see more or less everything from God's point of view, then we always seek and find opportunities to help others.

In Brazil lives a very simple woman. She loves the Lord. Her friends went every week to a women's prison to take the gospel through preaching, singing, and counseling. She could not do such things, but she had a love in her heart!

One thing she knew well: baking cakes. She suggested to her friends that she go with them and take a cake with her. I got an invitation to speak there and I will never forget it. All the women in this prison came. The beginning was not pleasant. We were searched by the guards, our bags were opened, and they fingered our clothes in case we had hidden something. But after that the women who had come with me started to sing hymns and I brought the Word. Then when we were through with everything, the moment came that seemed to be the climax for the prisoners.

Our friend brought in the cake she had made. She had taken a knife with her and cut the cake in many little pieces. She had also brought along little pieces of paper in many different colors. Every piece of cake was nicely packed and offered to the women. In the love of her heart she had understood what colors mean for prisoners. It was a feast, a real feast; everyone was happy.

Every week she did that and the women knew and counted on it, that after the preaching of the gospel this little treat came, too. This simple, faithful woman will one day hear, "I was in prison and you came to Me and gave Me cake."

In Australia I was at a big meeting and at the end I invited the people who wanted to be saved to come forward. The first who came were two little girls. I had told the people that they could go to a room behind the altar, but these children had not understood that. They stopped in front of me and one asked with a very clear little voice, so everyone in the church heard, "Am I too small to ask Jesus to come into my heart?"

"No, not at all," I said. "Jesus was interested even in the sparrow and you are much bigger than a sparrow! Jesus said, 'Let the little children come unto Me!' I was five years old when I asked Jesus to come into my heart and He came in and has never left me."

Then the little girl said aloud, so the whole church could hear it: "Lord Jesus, I have been very naughty. Will You come into my heart and cleanse it with Your blood?" And Jesus came in.

"What is your age?" I said to the other little girl: "Will you do the same?"

Then the little one said, "I did it three weeks ago and after that I prayed every day for Betty, and now Betty has done it!"

"Then you must pray together for a third girl," I said.

They looked at each other very thoughtfully and said at the same moment, "Anne. That must be Anne!" And then they promised to pray for Anne, until the Lord would knock at her heart and when Anne opened her heart for Jesus, they would pray together with Anne for a fourth girl, and so on.

This is the chain reaction of the gospel which started in the hearts of two little girls, who were not yet eight years old. This chain reaction of intercession can start in everyone's heart today!

—*Marching Orders for the End Battle*

QUESTIONS TO CONSIDER
1. Who could benefit from your act of service?
2. How can you serve this person as unto the Lord?

A PRAYERFUL RESPONSE
Lord, I will serve others as though I'm serving You. Amen.

PRAYING FOR REVIVAL

THOUGHT FOR TODAY

Praying for revival begins with spiritually stirring our own hearts.

WISDOM FROM SCRIPTURE

For we are God's servants, working together; you are God's field, God's building.

According to the grace of God given to me, like a skilled master builder I laid a foundation, and someone else is building on it. Each builder must choose with care how to build on it.

For no one can lay any foundation other than the one that has been laid; that foundation is Jesus Christ.

Now if anyone builds on the foundation with gold, silver, precious stones, wood, hay, straw—the work of each builder will become visible, for the Day will disclose it, because it will be revealed with fire, and the fire will test what sort of work each has done.

If what has been built on the foundation survives, the builder will receive a reward.

If the work is burned up, the builder will suffer loss; the builder will be saved, but only as through fire.

Do you not know that you are God's temple and that God's Spirit dwells in you?

If anyone destroys God's temple, God will destroy that person. For God's temple is holy, and you are that temple.

Do not deceive yourselves. If you think that you are wise in this age, you should become fools so that you may become wise.

For the wisdom of this world is foolishness with God.

1 CORINTHIANS 3:9-19, NRSV

INSIGHTS FROM CORRIE TEN BOOM

Can we rejoice in the resurrection life without having been crucified with Christ?

How much compromise there is!

I often wonder how it is possible that so many Christians live like beggars when we are royal children, the very children of God. We appropriate one or two of His promises, but most of them we negate or ignore or reject.

If indeed we have been "blessed...with all spiritual blessings in heavenly places in Christ" (Ephesians 1:3, KJV), why then do we still so often sigh? Are we really saved? Or is the devil right when he accuses us day and night? Is it true that we have been made the righteousness of God in Christ? (see 2 Corinthians 5:21).

Nietzsche has said, "Maybe I would have believed in a redeemer if the Christians had looked more redeemed." Is it not written in Romans 5:5: "The love of God is shed abroad in our hearts by the Holy Ghost which is given unto us" (KJV)? Why, then, do people not see that love in our eyes? We so often live like carnal Christians.

Are we to be saved by fire and our works burned?

This I do know, that we are living far below the level of what we actually are in Christ. How can this be? Is it perhaps that we do not really want to lose our lives for Christ's sake? If we want to save our lives we shall lose them.

May we then pray for a revival among others? What about our churches in this respect? Does my church rejoice to learn that a revival has started in another church which is perhaps much more fundamental or more modern than ours? Will they be glad to hear that twenty people have been converted in a particular group from which they differ so much?

No?

How, then, can my church pray for a revival?

And what about my readiness to forgive the sins of others? Are the sins of my sisters and brothers in Christ in the depths of the sea? Is the reputation of all absent persons safe in my keeping? Or are their sins so firmly anchored ashore that if you could ask me anything about them I can tell you immediately all about their irritating or unlovely characteristics?

If this be true of me, may I then pray for revival?

If I have so little understanding of the reality of God's promises that my problems seem greater than the victory of Christ, may I work toward a revival, even to the extent of praying for it?

Revive the world, O Lord, beginning with me!

—*Marching Orders for the End Battle*

QUESTIONS TO CONSIDER
1. How can you begin praying for revival?
2. Who might spend time praying with you?

A PRAYERFUL RESPONSE
Lord, let a spirit of revival begin in me. Amen.

THE STRENGTH OF JOY

THOUGHT FOR TODAY
The joy of the Lord can strengthen us.

WISDOM FROM SCRIPTURE
And Ezra opened the book in the sight of all the people, for he was standing above all the people; and when he opened it, all the people stood up.

Then Ezra blessed the Lord, the great God, and all the people answered, "Amen, Amen," lifting up their hands. Then they bowed their heads and worshiped the Lord with their faces to the ground.

And Nehemiah, who was the governor, and Ezra the priest and scribe, and the Levites who taught the people said to all the people, "This day is holy to the Lord your God; do not mourn or weep." For all the people wept when they heard the word of the law.

Then he said to them, "Go your way, eat the fat and drink sweet wine and send portions of them to those for whom nothing is prepared, for this day is holy to our Lord; and do not be grieved, for the joy of the Lord is your strength."

So the Levites stilled all the people, saying, "Be quiet, for this day is holy; do not be grieved."

And all the people went their way to eat and drink and to send portions and to make great rejoicing, because they had understood the words that were declared to them.

—NEHEMIAH 8:5-6, 9-12, NRSV

It is so important to know that in the final battle the joy of the Holy Spirit is available for us in all circumstances.

Once a prisoner wrote me a letter: *It is Christmas Eve. I am alone in my cell. There are no Christmas presents for me on the table. There is nothing that reminds me of Christmas. On the empty walls there are no Christmas decorations. But in my heart is Christmas joy, because Jesus lives there, and that is the greatest joy a human being can have. I could not send Corrie ten Boom a present, but I went on my knees and prayed for you for two hours. That was my Christmas present for you and it made my own heart still more joyful.*

I remember a dark day in Ravensbruck. Betsie and I talked much with the Lord. Horrible things happened around us. There were days we said to each other, "More terrible than today it can never be." But the next day was still more terrible. Despair was on all faces, for there was no salt in any of the meals that day. When you are slowly starving, salt is very important.

Several women died that day, one of them as a result of a cruel beating. The electric light had failed and after sunset we were in the deepest darkness. I put my arm around Betsie. She spoke about heaven and told me that shortly before we were arrested she had read about heaven in a booklet. We had a talk with the Lord. He spoke and we listened; then He listened while we spoke. Then we went to sleep under the dirty coat we used as a blanket, and Betsie said, "What a wonderful day we have had. The Lord has shown us so much of Himself."

When it rains in tropical countries, it really pours. I visited a prison in Rwanda. It was only a small building, but many prisoners were sitting outside on the ground.

"Where do you sleep at night?" I asked.

"Half of us sleep inside; the others must stay outside because there are too many prisoners." Some had a banana leaf, others had a branch or an old newspaper to sit on. The uniforms were gray, and the faces were dark and angry. It was all so sad.

Could I bring here the gospel, the tidings of great joy? No, I could not, but the Holy Spirit could. I prayed, "Lord, the fruit of the Spirit is joy. Give me an ocean of joy to share with these poor prisoners."

He did what I asked. I could almost shout for joy. I told them of a friend whose name is Jesus, who is good and so full of love, who never leaves you alone, who is strong and has the answer for all the great problems of sin and death. I said, "Perhaps you think, 'That is not for us, our lives are too terrible.' But I was in a prison where it was worse than here, where ninety-five thousand women were killed or died, including my own sister. There I experienced that Jesus is always with me. He lives in my heart; He has never left me alone."

I felt in my heart a great joy that imparted itself to the men who were sitting in the pouring rain. Then I saw that the joy of the Holy Spirit can be experienced in all circumstances. "This friend and Savior, Jesus, will live in your hearts," I continued. "Who will open the door of his heart to Him?" They all, including the guards, put up their hands, and their faces beamed.

My interpreter, a missionary, said, "I have been here once, but thought it was so hopeless that I stopped my visits. Now I have seen what the Holy Spirit can do. I will come here every week." She has done so, and the feast is going on!

—*Marching Orders for the End Battle*

QUESTIONS TO CONSIDER
1. Why would joy be able to strengthen us?
2. How can you receive God's joy today?

A PRAYERFUL RESPONSE
Lord, please fill me with Your joy and strength. Amen.

PART SIX

THE TIMES TO COME

I am not afraid when I think about the Coming of the Lord Jesus.
Instead, I welcome it. I do not know whether it would be better
for me to die and be among the great host of saints
who will return with Him, or whether it would be better to
remain here and listen for the sound of the trumpet.
Either way I like the words of the song that says:
God is working His purpose out,
As year succeeds to year:
God is working His purpose out
And the time is drawing near—
Nearer and nearer draws the time
The time that shall surely be,
When the earth shall be filled with the glory of God,
as the water covers the sea.

TRAMP FOR THE LORD

CORRIE TEN BOOM'S INSIGHT

We can prepare for Christ's Second Coming, but we need
not fear it.

DAY 36

SIGNS OF THE TIMES

THOUGHT FOR TODAY
Every day brings us closer to Christ's return.

WISDOM FROM SCRIPTURE
Now when he saw the crowds, he went up on a mountainside and sat down. His disciples came to him, and he began to teach them saying:

"Blessed are the poor in spirit,
for theirs is the kingdom of heaven.

"Blessed are those who mourn,
for they will be comforted.

"Blessed are the meek,
for they will inherit the earth.

"Blessed are those who hunger and thirst for
righteousness,
for they will be filled.

"Blessed are the merciful,
for they will be shown mercy.

"Blessed are the pure in heart,
for they will see God.

"Blessed are the peacemakers,
for they will be called sons of God.

"Blessed are those who are persecuted because of
righteousness,
for theirs is the kingdom of heaven.

"Blessed are you when people insult you, persecute you and falsely say all kinds of evil against you because of me.

"Rejoice and be glad, because great is your reward in

heaven, for in the same way they persecuted the prophets who were before you.

"You are the salt of the earth. But if the salt loses its saltiness, how can it be made salty again? It is no longer good for anything, except to be thrown out and trampled by men."   MATTHEW 5:1-13, NIV

INSIGHTS FROM CORRIE TEN BOOM

We live now in those days of which Jesus spoke. People are ready to know all about the weather conditions, but what about the signs of the times?

The end times have started already. Those who pay attention to the signs of the times will not doubt this at all. I believe everything that is written in the Bible about the coming again of Jesus. Everything that was written about the first coming of Jesus happened exactly as foretold, so that which is written about His coming again will happen.

This does not mean that I understand everything, but that is not necessary. We do not know the day, neither the hour, in which Jesus will come again. But neither do we know a day or an hour in which He could not come. The whole world lives now in this expectation; something must happen by which the great problems will be solved.

When we look at world history in the light of the Bible, we can find many clear signs. Luke 21:26 says, "Men will faint from fear and foreboding of what is coming upon the world." Everywhere in the world people are in great fear of an atomic war, and they are rightly afraid. There will be earthquakes, epidemics, and famines. "And because iniquity shall abound, the love of many shall wax cold" (Matthew 24:12, KJV). "Many shall run to and fro, and knowledge shall be increased" (Daniel 12:4, KJV). Just look at the development of space travel!

Mother Basilea Schlink says in her book *The End Is Coming:* "It may be true that this end-time has started, so that on the one side many things begin to be outlined on a larger scale, while on the other hand certain things about which we have been in the dark until now, become more clear, though on a smaller scale. Nevertheless, this does not alter the fact that very many details are still secret to us, and we have to wait for the hour that they will be brought to light."

The only thing we have to do, though, is what the Holy Scriptures teach us. We need to raise our voices like the voice of a trumpet so that as many people as possible will awake— first of all those who belong to the Church of Christ. We have to proclaim loudly that the end is near, so that people will be startled out of their everyday rest and security by this godly message, as through the roaring of the lion (see Amos 3:8); that they will fear and get ready to meet their God.

We urgently need such a "blowing of the trumpet" since the day of the Lord draws near, as the prophet Joel says: "Blow the trumpet in Zion, sanctify a fast, call a solemn assembly" (Joel 2:15, KJV). For we need to prepare ourselves for all that soon will come to pass.

But praise the Lord! "They that be with us are more than they that be with them" (2 Kings 6:16, KJV). The Syrian army that the servant of Elisha saw was a terrible, forbidding reality; but when his eyes were opened, he saw something far more important: the angels, a heavenly host with horses and chariots of fire, that had come to protect Elisha. And when we look at this invisible reality, then we know we stand on victory ground.

It is essential that we realize in these days that Jesus is conqueror! To stand at His side, to follow Him, to be hidden with Him in God—that is the safe position for every soldier of Jesus in this time and in the coming final battle.

—Marching Orders for the End Battle

QUESTIONS TO CONSIDER

1. When you think of the Lord's return, how do you feel?
2. How can you prepare for His return?

A PRAYERFUL RESPONSE

Lord, I wait expectantly for Your return to earth. Amen.

DAY 37

THE COMFORT OF GUIDANCE

THOUGHT FOR TODAY
The Lord promises to guide His children.

WISDOM FROM SCRIPTURE
I will instruct you and teach you in the way you should go;
> I will counsel you; and watch over you.

Do not be like the horse or the mule,
> which have no understanding

but must be controlled by bit and bridle
> or they will not come to you.

Many are the woes of the wicked,
> but the LORD'S unfailing love
> surrounds the man who trusts in him.

Rejoice in the LORD and be glad, you righteous;
> sing, all you who are upright in heart!

Yet the LORD longs to be gracious to you;
> he rises to show you compassion.

The LORD is a God of justice.
> Blessed are all who wait for him!

O people of Zion, who live in Jerusalem, you will weep no more. How gracious he will be when you cry for help! As soon as he hears, he will answer you.

Although the Lord gives you the bread of adversity and the water of affliction, your teachers will be hidden no more; with your own eyes you will see them.

Whether you turn to the right or to the left, your ears will hear a voice behind you, saying, "This is the way; walk in it."

The LORD will guide you always;

155

> he will satisfy your need in a sun-scorched land
> and will strengthen your frame.
> You will be like a well-watered garden,
> like a spring whose waters never fail.
>
> PSALMS 32:8-11; ISAIAH 30:18-21, 58:11, NIV

INSIGHTS FROM CORRIE TEN BOOM

A soldier has to know his marching orders; he must know where he has to go. It is so important at this time that we see the leading of the Lord very clearly.

People often ask me, "How can I know the will of God? How does the Lord lead His children?" We often make the words "surrender" and "leading" too complicated. When we discover what causes our view to be so dim, the meaning of these words becomes clear. There can be a fog around us, caused by the temptations of the enemy, but it is also possible that the "window" has become dirty on the inside by our sins. It can also happen that God puts His hands on the window, but especially then He is very close to us. We must get accustomed to and train ourselves to be guided by God.

The Holy Spirit makes us sensitive to His guidance. Often we must wait quietly, but waiting on the Lord can be a blessing in itself. We must learn to make our decisions in the presence of the Lord, when we are conscious of His nearness. Often God leads through the Bible; therefore we must know the Bible well. The better we know the Bible, the more His Word gives light on our path.

The Lord also leads us by our feelings. However, when we rely too much on our feelings, we can become too subjective; but it is not necessary that the leading of the Lord has nothing to do with our feelings. Just imagine someone telling you, "I have been married now for six months, but for some weeks I

156

have not felt that I am married." There is something wrong with that marriage.

God also uses our feelings to control our relations with Himself. The fruit of the Spirit is peace and joy, and that does not go without our feelings. Harmony with God goes together with harmony with Spirit-filled believers. Also in this we can find guidance. When God calls us His children, will He then not guide us safely as our Father?

God wants to take the lead in our lives. He longs for hidden fellowship with His children. He wants to teach us so that we get to know Him better. He will conform us to His image and will reach other people through us. But we can only bring His light to others when we are set apart for Him, sanctified. Sanctification means that God separates in our hearts light from darkness. The Holy Spirit brings us nearer to God and makes us conformable to Christ. He convicts us of sin, but He is also the Comforter and shows us Jesus. Then the separation between light and darkness comes into being. The devil accuses us to discourage us. Every feeling of guilt in our hearts we must confess immediately to the Lord, so that the vision gets clear again. "If the Son therefore shall make you free, ye shall be free indeed" (John 8:36, KJV).

The Lord leads us through His Word, through feelings, and through circumstances, and mostly through all three together. It is such a wonderful experience when the Lord speaks through our feelings and our thinking when we pray and listen to Him. The prayer then becomes a conversation from both sides. We on our side must also learn to expect that the Lord acts according to His promises and leads us on His way.

—*Marching Orders for the End Battle*

QUESTIONS TO CONSIDER
1. How do you know that God is guiding you?
2. What guidance do you need today?

A PRAYERFUL RESPONSE
Lord, guide me in Your path and plans. Amen.

FILLED AND FRUITFUL

THOUGHT FOR TODAY

The Holy Spirit fills us so we can be spiritually fruitful.

WISDOM FROM SCRIPTURE

You, my brothers, were called to be free. But do not use your freedom to indulge the sinful nature; rather, serve one another in love.

The entire law is summed up in a single command: "Love your neighbor as yourself."

If you keep on biting and devouring each other, watch out or you will be destroyed by each other.

So I say, live by the Spirit, and you will not gratify the desires of the sinful nature.

For the sinful nature desires what is contrary to the Spirit, and the Spirit what is contrary to the sinful nature. They are in conflict with each other, so that you do not do what you want.

But if you are led by the Spirit, you are not under law.

But the fruit of the Spirit is love, joy, peace, patience, kindness, goodness, faithfulness, gentleness and self-control. Against such things there is no law.

Those who belong to Christ Jesus have crucified the sinful nature with its passions and desires.

Since we live by the Spirit, let us keep in step with the Spirit. GALATIANS 5:13-18, 22-25, NIV

Insights from Corrie ten Boom

He who is filled with the Holy Spirit goes relaxed through life, for he knows that it is not a matter of trying but of trusting and yielding to Him "who shall also confirm you unto the end, that ye may be blameless in the day of our Lord Jesus Christ" (1 Corinthians 1:8, KJV).

It is the Lord Jesus Christ Himself who by His Spirit makes us live sanctified lives. He makes us obedient to what the Bible says: "But whatever happens, make sure that your everyday life is worthy of the gospel of Christ. So that whether I do come and see you, or merely hear about you from a distance, I may know that you are standing fast in a united spirit, battling with a single mind for the faith of the gospel and not caring two straws for your enemies" (Philippians 1:27-28).

Jesus is victor! He has conquered Satan, the power of sin, and the world. He that is in you, in me, is victor! We cannot overcome the enemy. We are powerless in ourselves. We are crucified with Christ, but also resurrected with Him unto a new life, here and now. It is the Lord Himself who accomplishes this. When we know this, we can see God's way, even when we have to go the hard way.

"We know that all things work together for good to them that love God" (Romans 8:28, KJV). It is by the grace of God that we can be conquerors. To be a conqueror, we must allow God to live His life in and through us. Again and again He has to break us; that is to say, He breaks the things in us that protect and maintain "self."

We must surrender totally to Him, and let Him do all that is necessary; thus He gets more and more room in us. He does not want only a part of us, but to fill our whole heart with His power, to fill us more and more with Himself. That means a closer fellowship with Him. That is glory!

When we are totally emptied of ourselves, we can be full of the Holy Spirit. Then we are conquerors and are able to accept all things from His hand. Besides this, we are being prepared to inherit all things. "And every man that hath this hope in him purifieth himself, even as He is pure" (1 John 3:3, KJV).

The contrasts between the Holy Spirit and self become more and more acute. But the Bible has a mighty answer: It is possible to be cleansed. No trying, no striving, but trusting in Him, looking unto Him in His Word, in our prayers, in our fellowship with Him. Then He cleanses us through His Word, that we bring forth more fruit as a branch on the vine. Jesus said, "I am the true vine, and my Father is the husbandman. Every branch that beareth fruit, he purgeth it, that it may bring forth more fruit" (John 15:1-2, KJV).

We cannot direct the knife with which He is going to purge us. It is to no purpose when we ourselves cut off a bit here and purge some there. The knife is in His hand, in the hand of the husbandman. He will cleanse and sanctify us.

—Marching Orders for the End Battle

QUESTIONS TO CONSIDER
1. What is your understanding of being filled with the Spirit?
2. Have you been filled with the Spirit? How do you know?

A PRAYERFUL RESPONSE
Lord, fill me with Your Holy Spirit so I can be spiritually fruitful. Amen.

MARTYRS FOR CHRIST

THOUGHT FOR TODAY
God gives us peace and power for our suffering.

WISDOM FROM SCRIPTURE
But we have this treasure in jars of clay to show that this all-surpassing power is from God and from us.

We are hard pressed on every side, but not crushed; perplexed, but not in despair; persecuted, but not abandoned; struck down, but not destroyed.

We always carry around in our body the death of Jesus, so that the life of Jesus may also be revealed in our body.

For we who are alive are always being given over to death for Jesus' sake, so that his life may be revealed in our mortal body.

So then, death is at work in us, but life is at work in you.

It is written: "I believed; therefore I have spoken."

With that same spirit of faith we also believe and therefore speak, because we know that the one who raised the Lord Jesus from the dead will also raise us with Jesus and present us with you in his presence.

All this is for your benefit, so that the grace that is reaching more and more people may cause thanksgiving to overflow to the glory of God.

Therefore we do not lose heart.

Though outwardly we are wasting away, yet inwardly we are being renewed day by day.

For our light and momentary troubles are achieving for us an eternal glory that far outweighs them all.

So we fix our eyes not on what is seen, but on what is

unseen. For what is seen is temporary, but what is unseen is eternal.

—2 CORINTHIANS 4:7-18, NIV

INSIGHTS FROM CORRIE TEN BOOM

I remember as a child saying to my father, "I am afraid I will never be strong enough to die as a martyr."

But he said, "When you have to go on a journey, when do I give you the money for the fare—two weeks before?"

"No, Daddy, on the day I am leaving."

"Precisely, and that is what the Savior does also."

He does not give us grace now for something we may have to pass through later on. If He thinks we are worthy to die as a martyr, He gives us the strength for it at that moment.

Once I was in Burundi. A civil war had broken out there. Every day people were imprisoned, including Christians. At night we heard shooting when many were killed. The children of God were in uncertainty. What would the future bring? On Sunday morning I spoke in a church. One could really feel the tension. Who would be arrested this week and killed? Who would still be alive next Sunday?

Then I spoke on 2 Corinthians 4:17 (KJV): "For our light affliction, which is but for a moment, worketh for us a far more exceeding and eternal weight of glory." I told them of an experience I had gone through myself.

When I was in a concentration camp during the war, the Bible was called the book of lies. It was a miracle that I still had my Bible. The room in which we lived with seven hundred women was so dirty that we were all full of lice. The guards and the other officials would never enter our room because they were afraid to get vermin from us. God can use even lice, for that is why I could bring a message from God's Word twice a day.

One day we got a new supervisor whose name was Lony. She was a prisoner, a cruel woman; she told the guards everything we did. One day I opened my Bible. A friend of mine said, "Don't do it today. Lony is sitting behind you. If she knows you have a Bible, she will see to it that you will be killed in a cruel way."

I prayed, "God give me the strength even now to bring Your Word." He answered that prayer. I read the Bible, brought the message, prayed, and then we sang, "Commit thy ways unto the Lord." When the song had finished, we heard someone call, "Another song like that!" It was Lony; she had enjoyed the singing. Afterward I got a chance to explain the gospel to her, to show her the way of salvation.

I am not a hero. When you know that what you are saying can mean a cruel death, then every word is as heavy as lead. But I have never had such joy and peace in my heart as when I gave that message, neither before that time, nor afterward. God gave me grace to be a martyr. Now I know from experience that when God demands it of us, when He thinks we are worthy to be martyrs, He will also give us grace.

When I told the church this story, a great joy came into the hearts of these people. Perhaps I must say it was a sad joy. Everyone knew it could be the last time they were assembled. But I felt as one does when one is at the deathbed of a child of God. Suddenly one sees the things of this world from God's point of view, the light of eternity. It gives a feeling of a certain freedom. One sees the great things great, the small things small. The things that are important in everyday life suddenly become very unimportant.

What, then, is important? The important things are the texts in God's Word, especially those that speak of heaven. For instance, where Jesus says, "In my Father's house are many mansions: if it were not so, I would have told you"

(John 14:2, KJV). Important is what is written about the glory of heaven: "O death, where is thy sting?" (1 Corinthians 15:55, KJV). I thank my God for the victory through Jesus Christ! "While we look not at the things which are seen, but at the things which are not seen: for the things which are seen are temporal; but the things which are not seen are eternal" (2 Corinthians 4:18, KJV).

I told them that when we are found worthy to die as martyrs, martyrs' crowns are awaiting us. Eternity is long, but time is short.

In that same week, many members of that church were arrested and martyred.

It is necessary when we prepare ourselves for the end times, also to be prepared to die for Jesus.

—Marching Orders for the End Battle

QUESTIONS TO CONSIDER

1. What are your fears about martyrdom?
2. How can you pray for the martyrs around the world?

A PRAYERFUL RESPONSE

Lord, I want to be willing to die for You. Amen.

JESUS IS VICTOR

THOUGHT FOR TODAY
Jesus Christ is our victor over the world.

WISDOM FROM SCRIPTURE
But now, this is what the LORD says—
> he who created you, O Jacob,
> he who formed you, O Israel;
"Fear not, for I have redeemed you;
> I have summoned you by name; you are mine.
> When you pass through the waters,
>> I will be with you;
> and when you pass through the rivers,
>> they will not sweep over you.
> When you walk through the fire,
>> you will not be burned;
>> the flames will not set you ablaze.
> For I am the LORD, your God,
>> the Holy One of Israel, your Savior;
> I give Egypt for your ransom,
>> Cush and Seba in your stead.
> Since you are precious and honored in my sight,
>> and because I love you,
> I will give men in exchange for you,
>> and people in exchange for your life.
> Do not be afraid, for I am with you."

Since you have kept my command to endure patiently, I will also keep you from the hour of trial that is going to come upon the whole world to test those who live on the earth.

I am coming soon.

Hold on to what you have, so that no one will take your crown.

—Isaiah 43:1-5; Revelation 3:10-11, NIV

Insights from Corrie ten Boom

The Lord Jesus demands much of us. He said, "For I say unto you, That except your righteousness shall exceed the righteousness of the scribes and Pharisees, ye shall in no case enter into the kingdom of heaven" (Matthew 5:20, KJV).

Nowadays people are inclined to belittle God. It is as if they look through the wrong end of a telescope. Their knowledge seems to be unlimited. God is far away and small, for many no longer to be seen. The possibilities for man are indeed unlimited, but only when he does not limit the promises of God through his unbelief. As the mountains and the stars of heaven are unshakable, so the works of Jesus are standing firm as a rock, and even more so, because they bear the stamp for eternity.

"Fear not: for I have redeemed thee, I have called thee by thy name; thou art mine. When thou passest through the waters, I will be with thee; and through the rivers, they shall not overflow thee: when thou walkest through the fire, thou shalt not be burned; neither shall the flame kindle upon thee. For I am the LORD thy God, the Holy One of Israel, thy Saviour" (Isaiah 43:1-3, KJV).

The presence of the Lord is our great comfort. With Jesus, hidden in God. He invites us to abide in Him. Be strong against a world full of unbelief, without being ashamed for your King. We must be Spirit-filled soldiers and must fight to gain the victory until Jesus comes. He is our strength now and also in the last battle.

"In all these things we win an overwhelming victory

through him who has proved his love for us" (Romans 8:37).

Hallelujah!

Jesus was victor!

Jesus is victor!

Jesus will be victor!

"He humbled himself by living a life of utter obedience, even to the extent of dying, and the death he died was the death of a common criminal. That is why God has now lifted him so high, and has given him the name beyond all names, so that at the name of Jesus every knee shall bow, whether in heaven or earth or under the earth. And that is why, in the end, every tongue shall confess that Jesus Christ is the Lord, to the glory of God the Father" (Philippians 2:8-11).

That is why we stand with Jesus through the Holy Spirit on victory ground. When you kneel before Him, will He be your Judge or your Savior?

—Marching Orders for the End Battle

QUESTIONS TO CONSIDER

1. Are you living in Christ's victory? Why or why not?
2. How can you walk in victory today?

A PRAYERFUL RESPONSE

Lord, thank You that I have victory in You. Amen.

BOOKS BY CORRIE TEN BOOM

A Prisoner and Yet...
A Tramp Finds a Home
Amazing Love
Anywhere He Leads Me
Christmas Memories
Clippings from My Notebook
Common Sense Not Needed
Defeated Enemies
Don't Wrestle, Just Nestle
Each New Day
Father ten Boom, God's Man
He Cares, He Comforts
He Sets the Captive Free
In My Father's House
Jesus Is Victor
Marching Orders for the End Battle
Not Good If Detached
Plenty for Everyone
Prayers and Promises for Every Day from the Living Bible
Snowflakes in September
The Hiding Place (with John and Elizabeth Sherrill)
This Day Is the Lord's
To God Be the Glory
Tramp for the Lord (with Jamie Buckingham)

About the Compiler

With the *Life Messages of Great Christians* series, Judith Couchman hopes you'll be encouraged and enlightened by people who've shared their spiritual journeys through the printed word.

Judith owns Judith & Company, an editorial consulting and writing business. She has been the creator and founding editor-in-chief of *Clarity* magazine, managing editor of *Christian Life*, editor of *Sunday Digest*, director of communications for The Navigators, and director of new product development for NavPress.

Besides speaking to women's and professional conferences, Judith has written or compiled fourteen books and many magazine articles. In addition, she has received numerous awards for her work in secondary education, religious publishing, and corporate communications.

She lives in Colorado.